God's Promises®
for Women
Catholic Edition

God's Promises® for Women
Catholic Edition

Edited by

Sr. Mary Ann Strain, C.P.
Rev. Victor Hoagland, C.P.

Regina Press
New York

ISBN# 0-88271-073-7

Printed in the United States of America.

THE REGINA PRESS
10 Hub Drive
Melville, New York 11747

❧ *Contents* ❧

God Walks with Women...

God Encourages Each Woman to...

God Teaches a Woman How to...

God Blesses Women When They...

God Comforts Women as They Learn to...

God Gives Freely to Women...

God Helps Women to Grow by...

God Rejoices with Women When They...

Dynamic Women of Faith

God's Plan for Women Is to …
Worship Him ❧

Give to the LORD, you heavenly beings,
   give to the LORD glory and might;
Give to the LORD the glory due God's name.
   Bow down before the LORD's holy splendor!
Psalm 29:1b–2

Enter, let us bow down in worship;
   let us kneel before the LORD who made us.
For this is our God,
   whose people we are,
   God's well-tended flock.

Oh, that today you would hear his voice.
Psalm 95:6–7

But the hour is coming, and is now here, when true worshippers will worship the Father in Spirit and truth; and indeed the Father seeks such people to worship him. God is Spirit, and those who worship him must worship in Spirit and truth.
John 4:23–24

Bow down to the LORD, splendid in holiness.
Tremble before God, all the earth.

Psalm 96:9

When you call me, when you go to pray to me,
I will listen to you. When you look for me, you will
find me. Yes, when you seek me with all your heart.
Jeremiah 29:12–13

Look to the LORD in his strength;
　seek to serve him constantly.
Recall the wondrous deeds that he has wrought,
　his portents, and the judgments he has uttered.
1 Chronicles 16:11–12

Happy those who observe God's decrees,
　who seek the LORD with all their heart.
With all my heart I seek you;
　do not let me stray from your commands.
Psalm 119:2, 10

I will bless you as long as I live;
　I will lift up my hands, calling on your name.
My soul shall savor the rich banquet of praise,
　with joyous lips my mouth shall honor you!
Psalm 63:5–6

God's Plan for Women Is to . . .
Obey Him ✒

Be doers of the word and not hearers only,
deluding yourselves.

James 1:22

If you love me, you will keep my
commandments.

John 14:15

But Peter and the apostles said in reply, "We
must obey God rather than men."

Acts 5:29

I will show you what someone is like who
comes to me, listens to my words, and acts on
them. That one is like a person building a house,
who dug deeply and laid the foundation on rock;
when the flood came, the river burst against that
house but could not shake it because it had been
well built. But the one who listens and does not act
is like a person who built a house on the ground
without a foundation. When the river burst against
it, it collapsed at once and was completely
destroyed.

Luke 6:47–49

The person who is trustworthy in very small matters is also trustworthy in great ones; and the person who is dishonest in very small matters is also dishonest in great ones.

Luke 16:10

Besides this, we have had our earthly fathers to discipline us, and we respected them. Should we not [then] submit all the more to the Father of spirits and live? They disciplined us for a short time as seemed right to them, but he does so for our benefit, in order that we may share his holiness.

Hebrews 12:9–10

Yet the world and its enticement are passing away. But whoever does the will of God remains forever.

1 John 2:17

But my just one shall live by faith,
and if he draws back I take no pleasure in him.

Hebrews 10:38

God's Plan for Women Is to ...
Come to Him in Prayer ℘

So let us confidently approach the throne of grace to receive mercy and to find grace for timely help.

Hebrews 4:16

At dusk, dawn, and noon
  I will grieve and complain,
  and my prayer will be heard.

Psalm 55:18

LORD, hear my prayer;
  listen to my cry for help.
In this time of trouble I call,
  for you will answer me.

Psalm 86:6–7

For the eyes of the Lord are on the righteous
  and his ears turned to their prayer,
  but the face of the Lord is against evildoers.
1 Peter 3:12

Then he told them a parable about the necessity for them to pray always without becoming weary.
Luke 18:1

When you pray, do not be like the hypocrites, who love to stand and pray in the synagogues and on street corners so that others may see them. Amen, I say to you, they have received their reward. But when you pray, go to your inner room, close the door, and pray to your Father in secret. And your Father who sees in secret will repay you.

Matthew 6:5–6

You shall entreat him and he will hear you,
   and your vows you shall fulfill.
When you make a decision, it shall succeed for you,
   and upon your ways the light shall shine.

Job 22:27–28

But he should ask in faith, not doubting, for the one who doubts is like a wave of the sea that is driven and tossed about by the wind.

James 1:6

God's Plan for Women Is to . . .
Listen to the Holy Spirit ✍

Among human beings, who knows what pertains to a person except the spirit of the person that is within? Similarly, no one knows what pertains to God except the Spirit of God. We have not received the spirit of the world but the Spirit that is from God, so that we may understand the things freely given us by God. And we speak about them not with words taught by human wisdom, but with words taught by the Spirit, describing spiritual realities in spiritual terms.

1 Corinthians 2:11–13

For the holy Spirit will teach you at that moment what you should say.

Luke 12:12

Rather, living the truth in love, we should grow in every way into him who is the head, Christ, from whom the whole body, joined and held together by every supporting ligament, with the proper functioning of each part, brings about the body's growth and builds itself up in love.

And do not grieve the holy Spirit of God, with which you were sealed for the day of redemption.

Ephesians 4:15–16, 30

But you, beloved, build yourselves up in your most holy faith; pray in the holy Spirit. Keep yourselves in the love of God and wait for the mercy of our Lord Jesus Christ that leads to eternal life.

Jude 20–21

"But I tell you the truth, it is better for you that I go. For if I do not go, the Advocate will not come to you. But if I go, I will send him to you. And when he comes he will convict the world in regard to sin and righteousness and condemnation: sin, because they do not believe in me; righteousness, because I am going to the Father and you will no longer see me; condemnation, because the ruler of this world has been condemned.

"I have much more to tell you, but you cannot bear it now."

John 16:7–12

Know this first of all, that there is no prophecy of scripture that is a matter of personal interpretation, for no prophecy ever came through human will; but rather human beings moved by the holy Spirit spoke under the influence of God.

2 Peter 1:20–21

If the Spirit of the one who raised Jesus from

the dead dwells in you, the one who raised Christ from the dead will give life to your mortal bodies also, through his Spirit that dwells in you.

The Spirit itself bears witness with our spirit that we are children of God, and if children, then heirs, heirs of God and joint heirs with Christ, if only we suffer with him so that we may also be glorified with him.

I consider that the sufferings of this present time are as nothing compared with the glory to be revealed for us.

In the same way, the Spirit too comes to the aid of our weakness; for we do not know how to pray as we ought, but the Spirit itself intercedes with inexpressible groanings. And the one who searches hearts knows what is the intention of the Spirit, because it intercedes for the holy ones according to God's will.

Romans 8:11, 16–18, 26–27

The Advocate, the holy Spirit that the Father will send in my name—he will teach you everything and remind you of all that [I] told you.

John 14:26

While meeting with them, he enjoined them not to depart from Jerusalem, but to wait for "the promise of the Father about which you have heard me speak; for John baptized with water, but in a few days you will be baptized with the holy Spirit."

He answered them, "It is not for you to know the times or seasons that the Father has established by his own authority. But you will receive power when the holy Spirit comes upon you, and you will be my witnesses in Jerusalem, throughout Judea and Samaria, and to the ends of the earth."

Acts 1:4–5, 7–8

Not that of ourselves we are qualified to take credit for anything as coming from us; rather, our qualification comes from God, who has indeed qualified us as ministers of a new covenant, not of letter but of spirit; for the letter brings death, but the Spirit gives life.

Now the Lord is the Spirit, and where the Spirit of the Lord is, there is freedom. All of us, gazing with unveiled face on the glory of the Lord, are being transformed into the same image from glory to glory, as from the Lord who is the Spirit.

2 Corinthians 3:5–6, 17–18

God Teaches Women to Walk in His Word by . . .
Praising His Might ❧

Hallelujah!
Sing to the LORD a new song,
   a hymn in the assembly of the faithful.

Psalm 149:1

Hallelujah!
Give thanks to the LORD, who is good,
   whose love endures forever.
Who can tell the mighty deeds of the LORD,
   proclaim in full God's praise?

Psalm 106:1–2

Hallelujah!
Praise, you servants of the LORD,
   praise the name of the LORD.
Blessed be the name of the LORD
   both now and forever.
From the rising of the sun to its setting
   let the name of the LORD be praised.

Psalm 113:1–3

That I may praise God's name in song
   and glorify it with thanksgiving.

Psalm 69:31

My heart is steadfast, God,
  my heart is steadfast.
  I will sing and chant praise.
Awake, my soul;
  awake, lyre and harp!
  I will wake the dawn.
I will praise you among the peoples, Lord;
  I will chant your praise among the nations.

Psalm 57:8–10

Hallelujah!
Praise the LORD, my soul;
  I shall praise the LORD all my life,
  sing praise to my God while I live.

Psalm 146:1–2

Great is the LORD and highly praised
  in the city of our God:
The holy mountain.

Psalm 48:2

All good giving and every perfect gift is from above, coming down from the Father of lights, with whom there is no alteration or shadow caused by change.

James 1:17

For your love is better than life;

my lips offer you worship!

I will bless you as long as I live;
   I will lift up my hands, calling on your name.
My soul shall savor the rich banquet of praise,
   with joyous lips my mouth shall honor you!

Psalm 63:4–6

God Teaches Women to Walk in His Word by . . .
Trusting His Power ✍

Before they call, I will answer;
while they are yet speaking, I will hearken to them.
Isaiah 65:24

"A nation of firm purpose you keep in peace;
  in peace, for its trust in you."

Trust in the LORD forever!
  For the LORD is an eternal Rock.
Isaiah 26:3–4

God indeed is my savior;
  I am confident and unafraid.
My strength and my courage is the LORD,
  and he has been my savior.
Isaiah 12:2

The LORD is with me; I am not afraid;
  what can mortals do against me?
Better to take refuge in the LORD
  than to put one's trust in mortals.
Psalm 118:6, 8

In you, LORD, I take refuge;
  let me never be put to shame.
You are my hope, Lord;
  my trust, GOD, from my youth.
My mouth shall be filled with your praise,
  shall sing your glory every day.

Psalm 71:1, 5, 8

Indeed, we had accepted within ourselves the sentence of death, that we might trust not in ourselves but in God who raises the dead. He rescued us from such great danger of death, and he will continue to rescue us; in him we have put our hope [that] he will also rescue us again.

2 Corinthians 1:9–10

They shall not fear an ill report;
  their hearts are steadfast, trusting the LORD.
Their hearts are tranquil, without fear,
  till at last they look down on their foes.

Psalm 112:7–8

The salvation of the just is from the LORD,
  their refuge in time of distress.
The LORD helps and rescues them,
  rescues and saves them from the wicked,
  because in God they take refuge.

Psalm 37:39–40

God Teaches Women to Walk
in His Word by . . .
Focusing on His Love ॐ

For thus said the Lord GOD,
 the Holy One of Israel:
By waiting and by calm you shall be saved,
 in quiet and in trust your strength lies.
 But this you did not wish.

Isaiah 30:15

Majestic and glorious is your work,
 your wise design endures forever.
You won renown for your wondrous deeds;
 gracious and merciful is the LORD.

Psalm 111:3–4

  So we are always courageous, although we
know that while we are at home in the body we are
away from the Lord, for we walk by faith, not by
sight.

2 Corinthians 5:6–7

Fear not, I am with you;
 be not dismayed; I am your God.
I will strengthen you, and help you,
 and uphold you with my right hand of justice.

Isaiah 41:10

God is our refuge and our strength,
   an ever-present help in distress.
Thus we do not fear, though earth be shaken
   and mountains quake to the depths of the sea,
Though its waters rage and foam
   and mountains totter at its surging.

Psalm 46:2–4a

They were hungry and thirsty;
   their life was ebbing away.
In their distress they cried to the LORD,
   who rescued them in their peril,
Guided them by a direct path
   so they reached a city to live in.

Psalm 107:5–7

For God did not give us a spirit of cowardice but rather of power and love and self-control. He saved us and called us to a holy life, not according to our works but according to his own design and the grace bestowed on us in Christ Jesus before time began.

2 Timothy 1:7, 9

Come to me, all you who labor and are burdened, and I will give you rest. Take my yoke upon you and learn from me, for I am meek and humble of heart; and you will find rest for your selves. For my yoke is easy, and my burden light.

Matthew 11:28–30

For he has said, "I will never forsake you or abandon you."

Hebrews 13:5b

The same night the LORD appeared to him and said: "I am the God of your father Abraham. You have no need to fear, since I am with you. I will bless you and multiply your descendants for the sake of my servant Abraham."

Genesis 26:24

God Teaches Women to Walk in His Word by . . .
Praying for His Will ♨

At dusk, dawn, and noon
  I will grieve and complain,
  and my prayer will be heard.

Psalm 55:18

Even after Daniel heard that this law had been signed, he continued his custom of going home to kneel in prayer and give thanks to his God in the upper chamber three times a day, with the windows open toward Jerusalem.

Daniel 6:11

Seven times a day I praise you
  because your edicts are just.

Psalm 119:164

I will ponder your precepts
  and consider your paths.
In your laws I take delight;
  I will never forget your word.

Psalm 119:15–16

Your word is a lamp for my feet,

a light for my path.

Psalm 119:105

Thus faith comes from what is heard, and what is heard comes through the word of Christ.

Romans 10:17

But those sown on rich soil are the ones who hear the word and accept it and bear fruit thirty and sixty and a hundredfold.

Mark 4:20

The LORD is far from the wicked,
  but the prayer of the just he hears.

Proverbs 15:29

Pray without ceasing.

1 Thessalonians 5:17

God Teaches Women to Walk in His Word by . . .
Following His Light ✍

For the bidding is a lamp, and the teaching a light,
and a way to life are the reproofs of discipline.

Proverbs 6:23

Be eager to present yourself as acceptable to God, a workman who causes no disgrace, imparting the word of truth without deviation.

2 Timothy 2:15

In my heart I treasure your promise,
that I may not sin against you.
Blessed are you, O LORD;
teach me your laws.

Psalm 119:11–12

For "In him we live and move and have our being," as even some of your poets have said, "For we too are his offspring."

Acts 17:28

Anyone who is so "progressive" as not to remain in the teaching of the Christ does not have God; whoever remains in the teaching has the

Father and the Son.

2 John 1:9

Draw near to God, and he will draw near to you. Cleanse your hands, you sinners, and purify your hearts, you of two minds.

James 4:8

Jesus said to him, " 'If you can!' Everything is possible to one who has faith."

Mark 9:23

Now those who belong to Christ [Jesus] have crucified their flesh with its passions and desires. If we live in the Spirit, let us also follow the Spirit.

Galatians 5:24–25

God Teaches Women to Walk in His Word by . . .
Rejoicing Day and Night 🍃

How sweet to my tongue is your promise,
  sweeter than honey to my mouth!

Psalm 119:103

The law of the LORD is perfect,
  refreshing the soul.
The decree of the LORD is trustworthy,
  giving wisdom to the simple.
The precepts of the LORD are right,
  rejoicing the heart.
The command of the LORD is clear,
  enlightening the eye.
More desirable than gold,
  than a hoard of purest gold,
Sweeter also than honey
  or drippings from the comb.

Psalm 19:8–9, 11

Keep this book of the law on your lips. Recite it by
day and by night, that you may observe carefully
all that is written in it; then you will successfully
attain your goal.

Joshua 1:8

I will ponder your precepts
   and consider your paths.
In your laws I take delight;
   I will never forget your word.

Psalm 119:15–16

   You should put away the old self of your
former way of life, corrupted through deceitful
desires, and be renewed in the spirit of your minds,
and put on the new self, created in God's way in
righteousness and holiness of truth.

Ephesians 4:22–24

Therefore, we are not discouraged; rather, although
our outer self is wasting away, our inner self is
being renewed day by day.

2 Corinthians 4:16

At dawn may the LORD bestow faithful love
   that I may sing praise through the night,
   praise to the God of my life.

Psalm 42:9

God Delights in Women Who Are . . .
Seeking Him ☙

Even if my father and mother forsake me,
   the LORD will take me in.

Psalm 27:10

O God, you are my God—
   for you I long!
For you my body yearns;
   for you my soul thirsts,
Like a land parched, lifeless,
   and without water.

Psalm 63:2

Look to the LORD in his strength;
   seek to serve him constantly.
Recall the wondrous deeds that he has wrought,
   his portents, and the judgments he has uttered.

1 Chronicles 16:11–12

   For, if you confess with your mouth that Jesus
is Lord and believe in your heart that God raised
him from the dead, you will be saved.

Romans 10:9

Those who love me I also love,

and those who seek me find me.

Proverbs 8:17

Until I arrive, attend to the reading, exhortation, and teaching.

1 Timothy 4:13

Sometimes a way seems right to a man,
  but the end of it leads to death!

Proverbs 14:12

I sought the LORD, who answered me,
  delivered me from all my fears.

Psalm 34:5

Always seek what is good [both] for each other and for all.

1 Thesssalonians 5:15b

God Delights in Women Who Are . . .
Confident of Him ✍

I will not leave you orphans; I will come to you.
John 14:18

I give thanks to my God at every remembrance of you.
Philippians 1:3

In you, LORD, I take refuge;
   let me never be put to shame.
In your justice rescue and deliver me;
   listen to me and save me!
You are my hope, Lord;
   my trust, GOD, from my youth.
Psalm 71:1– 2, 5

Better to take refuge in the LORD
   than to put one's trust in mortals.
Psalm 118:8

The LORD will guard you from all evil,
   will always guard your life.
The LORD will guard your coming and going
   both now and forever.
Psalm 121:7–8

So submit yourselves to God. Resist the devil, and he will flee from you.

James 4:7

May grace and peace be yours in abundance through knowledge of God and of Jesus our Lord.

His divine power has bestowed on us everything that makes for life and devotion, through the knowledge of him who called us by his own glory and power. Through these, he has bestowed on us the precious and very great promises, so that through them you may come to share in the divine nature, after escaping from the corruption that is in the world because of evil desire.

2 Peter 1:2–4

Who [indeed] is the victor over the world but the one who believes that Jesus is the Son of God?

1 John 5:5

Jesus looked at them and said, "For human beings this is impossible, but for God all things are possible."

Matthew 19:26

God Delights in Women Who Are . . .
Forgiven by Him ❧

To the one who is able to keep you from stumbling and to present you unblemished and exultant, in the presence of his glory, to the only God, our savior, through Jesus Christ our Lord be glory, majesty, power, and authority from ages past, now, and for ages to come. Amen.

Jude 24–25

Hence, now there is no condemnation for those who are in Christ Jesus. For the law of the spirit of life in Christ Jesus has freed you from the law of sin and death.

Romans 8:1–2

If we acknowledge our sins, he is faithful and just and will forgive our sins and cleanse us from every wrongdoing.

1 John 1:9

You forgave the guilt of your people,
   pardoned all their sins.

Psalm 85:3

But the Lord is faithful; he will strengthen you and guard you from the evil one.

2 Thessalonians 3:3

Whomever you forgive anything, so do I. For indeed what I have forgiven, if I have forgiven anything, has been for you in the presence of Christ, so that we might not be taken advantage of by Satan, for we are not unaware of his purposes.

2 Corinthians 2:10–11

I will give the victor the right to sit with me on my throne, as I myself first won the victory and sit with my Father on his throne.

Revelation 3:21

The Lord will rescue me from every evil threat and will bring me safe to his heavenly kingdom. To him be glory forever and ever. Amen.

2 Timothy 4:18

God Delights in Women Who Are . . .
Growing in Him ✍

I will instruct you and show you the
    way you should walk,
    give you counsel and watch over you.

Psalm 32:8

Keep this book of the law on your lips. Recite it by day and by night, that you may observe carefully all that is written in it; then you will successfully attain your goal.

Joshua 1:8

So that we may no longer be infants, tossed by waves and swept along by every wind of teaching arising from human trickery, from their cunning in the interests of deceitful scheming. Rather, living the truth in love, we should grow in every way into him who is the head, Christ.

Ephesians 4:14–15

Be doers of the word and not hearers only, deluding yourselves.

James 1:22

I am the vine, you are the branches. Whoever

remains in me and I in him will bear much fruit, because without me you can do nothing.

John 15:5

O God, you are my God—
   for you I long!
For you my body yearns;
   for you my soul thirsts,
Like a land parched, lifeless,
   and without water.
So I look to you in the sanctuary
   to see your power and glory.

My soul shall savor the rich banquet of praise,
   with joyous lips my mouth shall honor you!
When I think of you upon my bed,
   through the night watches I will recall
That you indeed are my help,
   and in the shadow of your wings I shout for joy.

Psalm 63:2–3, 6–8

It was not you who chose me, but I who chose you and appointed you to go and bear fruit that will remain, so that whatever you ask the Father in my name he may give you.

John 15:16

God Delights in Women Who Are . . .
Serving Him ❧

If it does not please you to serve the LORD, decide today whom you will serve, the gods your fathers served beyond the River or the gods of the Amorites in whose country you are dwelling. As for me and my household, we will serve the LORD.

Joshua 24:15

Whoever serves me must follow me, and where I am, there also will my servant be. The Father will honor whoever serves me.

John 12:26

At this, Jesus said to him, "Get away, Satan! It is written:
'The Lord, your God, shall you worship
and him alone shall you serve.'"

Matthew 4:10

And the crowds asked him, "What then should we do?" He said to them in reply, "Whoever has two cloaks should share with the person who has none. And whoever has food should do likewise."

Luke 3:10–11

This is how all will know that you are my disciples, if you have love for one another.

John 13:35

Tell the rich in the present age not to be proud and not to rely on so uncertain a thing as wealth but rather on God, who richly provides us with all things for our enjoyment. Tell them to do good, to be rich in good works, to be generous, ready to share, thus accumulating as treasure a good foundation for the future, so as to win the life that is true life.

1 Timothy 6:17–19

Each one must examine his own work, and then he will have reason to boast with regard to himself alone, and not with regard to someone else; for each will bear his own load.

One who is being instructed in the word should share all good things with his instructor. Let us not grow tired of doing good, for in due time we shall reap our harvest, if we do not give up.

Galatians 6:4–6, 9

Then the people promised Joshua, "We will serve the LORD, our God, and obey his voice."

Joshua 24:24

God Delights in Women Who Are . . .
Showing Him to Others ᴓ

The way we may be sure that we know him is to keep his commandments. But whoever keeps his word, the love of God is truly perfected in him. This is the way we may know that we are in union with him.

1 John 2:3, 5

Therefore, since we have been justified by faith, we have peace with God through our Lord Jesus Christ, through whom we have gained access [by faith] to this grace in which we stand, and we boast in hope of the glory of God. Not only that, but we even boast of our afflictions, knowing that affliction produces endurance, and endurance, proven character, and proven character, hope.

Romans 5:1–4

Finally, draw your strength from the Lord and from his mighty power. Put on the armor of God so that you may be able to stand firm against the tactics of the devil.

Ephesians 6:10–11

What we have seen and heard

we proclaim now to you,
so that you too may have fellowship with us;
for our fellowship is with the Father
and with his Son, Jesus Christ.

1 John 1:3

Indeed someone might say, "You have faith and I have works." Demonstrate your faith to me without works, and I will demonstrate my faith to you from my works. You see that faith was active along with his works, and faith was completed by the works.

James 2:18, 22

Woe to the rebellious children,
  says the LORD,
Who carry out plans that are not mine,
  who weave webs that are not inspired by me,
    adding sin upon sin.

Isaiah 30:1

Know this, my dear brothers: everyone should be quick to hear, slow to speak, slow to wrath, for the wrath of a man does not accomplish the righteousness of God. Therefore, put away all filth and evil excess and humbly welcome the word that has been planted in you and is able to save your souls.

Religion that is pure and undefiled before God and the Father is this: to care for orphans and widows in their affliction and to keep oneself unstained by the world.

James 1:19–21, 27

Those sown among thorns are another sort. They are the people who hear the word, but worldly anxiety, the lure of riches, and the craving for other things intrude and choke the word, and it bears no fruit. But those sown on rich soil are the ones who hear the word and accept it and bear fruit thirty and sixty and a hundredfold.

Mark 4:18–20

Now if you invoke as Father him who judges impartially according to each one's works, conduct yourselves with reverence during the time of your sojourning, realizing that you were ransomed from your futile conduct, handed on by your ancestors, not with perishable things like silver or gold but with the precious blood of Christ as of a spotless unblemished lamb.

1 Peter 1:17-19

That is how we speak, not as trying to please human beings, but rather God, who judges our hearts.

1 Thessalonians 2:4b

God Walks with Women . . .
Through Heartache ॐ

Heals the brokenhearted,
  binds up their wounds.

Psalm 147:3

In his mind a man plans his course,
  but the LORD directs his steps.

When the lot is cast into the lap,
  its decision depends entirely on the LORD.

Proverbs 16:9, 33

The LORD is close to the brokenhearted,
  saves those whose spirit is crushed.
Many are the troubles of the just,
  but the LORD delivers from them all.

Psalm 34:19–20

  Come to me, all you who labor and are
burdened, and I will give you rest. Take my yoke
upon you and learn from me, for I am meek and
humble of heart; and you will find rest for
yourselves.

Matthew 11:28–29

Now will I rise up, says the LORD,
   now will I be exalted, now be lifted up.

Isaiah 33:10

The LORD is a stronghold for the oppressed,
   stronghold in times of trouble.
Those who honor your name trust in you;
   you never forsake those who seek you, LORD.

Psalm 9:10–11

When I cried out, you answered;
   you strengthened my spirit.

Psalm 138:3

Then the LORD will guide you always
   and give you plenty even on the parched land.
He will renew your strength,
   and you shall be like a watered garden,
   like a spring whose water never fails.

Isaiah 58:11

God Walks with Women . . .
Through Adversity ✍

The fear of man brings a snare,
  but he who trusts in the LORD is safe.

Proverbs 29:25

We will triumph with the help of God,
  who will trample down our foes.

Psalm 60:14

Beloved, do not be surprised that a trial by fire is occurring among you, as if something strange were happening to you. But rejoice to the extent that you share in the sufferings of Christ, so that when his glory is revealed you may also rejoice exultantly.

1 Peter 4:12–13

…and live to see your children's children.
Peace upon Israel!

Psalm 128:6

But thanks be to God, who always leads us in triumph in Christ and manifests through us the odor of the knowledge of him in every place.

2 Corinthians 2:14

My heart is steadfast, God,
  my heart is steadfast.
  I will sing and chant praise.

Psalm 57:8

But he said to me, "My grace is sufficient for you, for power is made perfect in weakness." I will rather boast most gladly of my weaknesses, in order that the power of Christ may dwell with me.

2 Corinthians 12:9

The LORD is with me to the end.
  LORD, your love endures forever.
  Never forsake the work of your hands!

Psalm 138:8

God Walks with Women . . .
Through Danger ✍

My soul, be at rest in God alone,
   from whom comes my hope.
God alone is my rock and my salvation,
   my secure height; I shall not fall.
My safety and glory are with God,
   my strong rock and refuge.

Psalm 62:6–8

Do not be my ruin,
   you, my refuge in the day of misfortune.

Jeremiah 17:17

When you pass through the water, I will be
         with you;
   in the rivers you shall not drown.
When you walk through fire, you shall not be
         burned;
   the flames shall not consume you.

Isaiah 43:2

Keep me as the apple of your eye;
   hide me in the shadow of your wings.

Psalm 17:8

Even when I walk through a dark valley,
   I fear no harm for you are at my side;
   your rod and staff give me courage.

Psalm 23:4

My wanderings you have noted;
   are my tears not stored in your vial,
   recorded in your book?
   in you I trust, I do not fear.
   What can mere mortals do to me?

Psalm 56:9, 12

The LORD raises the needy from the dust,
   lifts the poor from the ash heap,
Gives the childless wife a home,
   the joyful mother of children.
Hallelujah!

Psalm 113:7, 9

For God will hide me in his shelter
   in time of trouble,
Will conceal me in the cover of his tent;
   and set me high upon a rock.

Psalm 27:5

God Walks with Women . . .
Through Impatience 🍂

My soul looks for the Lord
  more than sentinels for daybreak.
More than sentinels for daybreak.

Psalm 130:6

Consider it all joy, my brothers, when you encounter various trials, for you know that the testing of your faith produces perseverance. And let perseverance be perfect, so that you may be perfect and complete, lacking in nothing.

James 1:2–4

Be patient, therefore, brothers, until the coming of the Lord. See how the farmer waits for the precious fruit of the earth, being patient with it until it receives the early and the late rains. You too must be patient. Make your hearts firm, because the coming of the Lord is at hand.

James 5:7–8

"I myself," the LORD answered, "will go along, to give you rest."

Exodus 33:14

Wait for the LORD, take courage;
  be stouthearted, wait for the LORD!

Psalm 27:14

They that hope in the LORD will renew their
    strength,
  they will soar as with eagles' wings;
They will run and not grow weary,
  walk and not grow faint.

Isaiah 40:31

Whenever I cried out to the LORD,
  I was answered from the holy mountain.
Whenever I lay down and slept,
  the LORD preserved me to rise again.

Psalm 3:5–6

  And so, after patient waiting, he obtained the
promise.

Hebrews 6:15

God Walks with Women . . .
Through Disappointment ✍

LORD, I call to you;
  come quickly to help me;
  listen to my plea when I call.
Let my prayer be incense before you;
  my uplifted hands an evening sacrifice.

Psalm 141:1b–2

  Many peoples shall come and say:
"Come, let us climb the LORD'S mountain,
  to the house of the God of Jacob,
That he may instruct us in his ways,
  and we may walk in his paths."
For from Zion shall go forth instruction,
  and the word of the LORD from Jerusalem.

Isaiah 2:3

Compete well for the faith. Lay hold of eternal life, to which you were called when you made the noble confession in the presence of many witnesses.

1 Timothy 6:12

Son though he was, he learned obedience from what he suffered.

Hebrews 5:8

I have competed well; I have finished the race; I have kept the faith. From now on the crown of righteousness awaits me, which the Lord, the just judge, will award to me on that day, and not only to me, but to all who have longed for his appearance.

2 Timothy 4:7–8

Indeed, religion with contentment is a great gain. For we brought nothing into the world, just as we shall not be able to take anything out of it. If we have food and clothing, we shall be content with that.

1 Timothy 6:6–8

I recognized that whatever God does will endure forever; there is no adding to it, or taking from it. Thus has God done that he may be revered.

Ecclesiastes 3:14

But the wisdom from above is first of all pure, then peaceable, gentle, compliant, full of mercy and good fruits, without inconstancy or insincerity.

James 3:17

For whenever anyone bears the pain of unjust suffering because of consciousness of God, that is a grace. But what credit is there if you are patient when beaten for doing wrong? But if you are patient when you suffer for doing what is good, this is a grace before God.

1 Peter 2:19–20

May our Lord Jesus Christ himself and God our Father, who has loved us and given us everlasting encouragement and good hope through his grace, encourage your hearts and strengthen them in every good deed and word.

2 Thessalonians 2:16, 17

It [love] bears all things, believes all things, hopes all things, endures all things.

1 Corinthians 13:7

God Walks with Women . . .
Through Failure Ꮬ᎒

Whoever loves his life loses it, and whoever hates his life in this world will preserve it for eternal life.

John 12:25

Think of what is above, not of what is on earth.

Colossians 3:2

Tell the rich in the present age not to be proud and not to rely on so uncertain a thing as wealth but rather on God, who richly provides us with all things for our enjoyment. Tell them to do good, to be rich in good works, to be generous, ready to share, thus accumulating as treasure a good foundation for the future, so as to win the life that is true life.

1 Timothy 6:17–19

Listen to counsel and receive instruction,
    that you may eventually become wise.

Proverbs 19:20

All this I have kept in mind and recognized: the just, the wise, and their deeds are in the hand of

God. Love from hatred man cannot tell; both appear equally vain.

Ecclesiastes 9:1

But you are "a chosen race, a royal priesthood, a holy nation, a people of his own, so that you may announce the praises" of him who called you out of darkness into his wonderful light.

1 Peter 2:9

Has not dealt with us as our sins merit,
  nor requited us as our deeds deserve.

As the heavens tower over the earth,
  so God's love towers over the faithful.
As far as the east is from the west,
  so far have our sins been removed from us.

Psalm 103:10–12

Cast your care upon the LORD,
  who will give you support.
God will never allow
  the righteous to stumble

Psalm 55:23

God Encourages Each Woman to . . .
Cherish Being a Friend ∿

Let mutual love continue. Do not neglect
hospitality, for through it some have unknowingly
entertained angels.

Hebrews 13:1–2

He who is a friend is always a friend,
   and a brother is born for the time of stress.

Proverbs 17:17

This is my commandment: love one another as
I love you. No one has greater love than this, to lay
down one's life for one's friends.

John 15:12–13

If [one] part suffers, all the parts suffer with it;
if one part is honored, all the parts share its joy.

1 Corinthians 12:26

Two are better than one: they get a good wage
for their labor.

Ecclesiastes 4:9

One man helps another,
   one says to the other, "Keep on!"

Isaiah 41:6

For whoever does the will of my heavenly Father is my brother, and sister, and mother.

Matthew 12:50

As a body is one though it has many parts, and all the parts of the body, though many, are one body, so also Christ.

1 Corinthians 12:12

Serve one another through love.

Galatians 5:13b

Your every act should be done with love.

1 Corinthians 16:14

God Encourages Each Woman to . . .
Give to Others with Grace ⌦

Let us not grow tired of doing good, for in due
time we shall reap our harvest, if we do not give
up.

Galatians 6:9

Give and gifts will be given to you; a good
measure, packed together, shaken down, and
overflowing, will be poured into your lap. For the
measure with which you measure will in return be
measured out to you.

Luke 6:38

She reaches out her hands to the poor,
and extends her arms to the needy.

Proverbs 31:20

He who gives to the poor suffers no want,
but he who ignores them gets many a curse.

Proverbs 28:27

Defend the lowly and fatherless;
render justice to the afflicted and needy.
Rescue the lowly and poor;
deliver them from the hand of the wicked.

Psalm 82:3–4

The way we came to know love was that he laid down his life for us; so we ought to lay down our lives for our brothers. If someone who has worldly means sees a brother in need and refuses him compassion, how can the love of God remain in him?

1 John 3:16–17

And whoever gives only a cup of cold water to one of these little ones to drink because he is a disciple—amen, I say to you, he will surely not lose his reward.

Matthew 10:42

You have been told, O man, what is good,
    and what the LORD requires of you:
Only to do right and to love goodness,
    and to walk humbly with your God.

Micah 6:8

Do not return evil for evil, or insult for insult; but, on the contrary, a blessing, because to this you were called, that you might inherit a blessing.

1 Peter 3:9

God Encourages Each Woman to . . .
Live a Life of Service ✍

Whoever is without love does not know God, for God is love.

1 John 4:8

And now, children, remain in him, so that when he appears we may have confidence and not be put to shame by him at his coming.

1 John 2:28

I give you a new commandment: love one another. As I have loved you, so you also should love one another. This is how all will know that you are my disciples, if you have love for one another.

John 13:34–35

Whoever wishes to be first among you shall be your slave. Just so, the Son of Man did not come to be served but to serve and to give his life as a ransom for many.

Matthew 20:27–28

For you were called for freedom, brothers. But do not use this freedom as an opportunity for the flesh; rather, serve one another through love.

Galatians 5:13

As each one has received a gift, use it to serve one another as good stewards of God's varied grace. Whoever preaches, let it be with the words of God; whoever serves, let it be with the strength that God supplies, so that in all things God may be glorified through Jesus Christ, to whom belong glory and dominion forever and ever. Amen.

1 Peter 4:10–11

Whatever you do, do from the heart, as for the Lord and not for others, knowing that you will receive from the Lord the due payment of the inheritance; be slaves of the Lord Christ. For the wrongdoer will receive recompense for the wrong he committed, and there is no partiality.

Colossians 3:23–25

The person who is trustworthy in very small matters is also trustworthy in great ones; and the person who is dishonest in very small matters is also dishonest in great ones. If, therefore, you are not trustworthy with dishonest wealth, who will trust you with true wealth? If you are not trustworthy with what belongs to another, who will give you what is yours? No servant can serve two masters. He will either hate one and love the other, or be devoted to one and despise the other. You cannot serve God and mammon.

Luke 16:10–13

God Encourages Each Woman to . . .
Offer Encouragement ✍

Rejoice with those who rejoice, weep with those who weep. Have the same regard for one another; do not be haughty but associate with the lowly; do not be wise in your own estimation.

Romans 12:15–16

Therefore, encourage one another and build one another up, as indeed you do.

1 Thessalonians 5:11

Let us then pursue what leads to peace and to building up one another.

Romans 14:19

We must consider how to rouse one another to love and good works. We should not stay away from our assembly, as is the custom of some, but encourage one another, and this all the more as you see the day drawing near.

Hebrews 10:24–25

But if we walk in the light as he is in the light, then we have fellowship with one another, and the blood of his Son Jesus cleanses us from all sin.

1 John 1:7

If then you were raised with Christ, seek what is above, where Christ is seated at the right hand of God. Think of what is above, not of what is on earth.

Colossians 3:1–2

You are my shelter; from distress you keep me;
  with safety you ring me round.

Psalm 32:7

Do not be afraid any longer, little flock, for your Father is pleased to give you the kingdom.

Luke 12:32

May the Lord of peace himself give you peace at all times and in every way. The Lord be with all of you.

2 Thessalonians 3:16

In this way the love of God was revealed to us: God sent his only Son into the world so that we might have life through him.

1 John 4:9

God Encourages Each Woman to . . .
Pray for One Another ✍

I am the LORD, the God of all mankind! Is anything impossible to me?

Jeremiah 32:27

Have among yourselves the same attitude that is also yours in Christ Jesus.

Philippians 2:5

"For the eyes of the Lord are on the righteous
    and his ears turned to their prayer,
but the face of the Lord is against evildoers."
    Now who is going to harm you if you are enthusiastic for what is good?

1 Peter 3:12–13

Rejoice always. Pray without ceasing. In all circumstances give thanks, for this is the will of God for you in Christ Jesus.

1 Thessalonians 5:16–18

And take the helmet of salvation and the sword of the Spirit, which is the word of God.

With all prayer and supplication, pray at every opportunity in the Spirit. To that end, be watchful with all perseverance and supplication for all the holy ones.

Ephesians 6:17–18

You belong to God, children, and you have conquered them, for the one who is in you is greater than the one who is in the world.

1 John 4:4

Away from me, all who do evil!
  The LORD has heard my weeping.
The LORD has heard my prayer;
  the LORD takes up my plea.

Psalm 6:9–10

LORD, hear my prayer;
  listen to my cry for help.
In this time of trouble I call,
  for you will answer me.

Psalm 86:6–7

And we have this confidence in him, that if we ask anything according to his will, he hears us. And if we know that he hears us in regard to whatever we ask, we know that what we have asked him for is ours.

1 John 5:14–15

God Encourages Each Woman to . . .
Celebrate with Joy ৯

I will praise you, LORD, with all my heart;
   I will declare all your wondrous deeds.
I will delight and rejoice in you;
   I will sing hymns to your name, Most High.
                                    Psalm 9:2–3

   On that day it will be said:
"Behold our God, to whom we looked to save us!
   This is the LORD for whom we looked;
   let us rejoice and be glad that he has saved us!"
                                    Isaiah 25:9

The promises of the LORD I will sing forever,
   proclaim your loyalty through all ages.
                                    Psalm 89:2

In your laws I take delight;
   I will never forget your word.

Make me understand the way of your precepts;
   I will ponder your wondrous deeds.
                                    Psalm 119:16, 27

A glad heart lights up the face,

but by mental anguish the spirit is broken.

Proverbs 15:13

Thus says the LORD: In this place of which you say, "How desolate it is, without man, without beast!" and in the cities of Judah, in the streets of Jerusalem that are now deserted, without man, without citizen, without beast, there shall yet be heard the cry of joy, the cry of gladness, the voice of the bridegroom, the voice of the bride, the sound of those who bring thank offerings to the house of the LORD, singing, "Give thanks to the LORD of hosts, for the LORD is good; his mercy endures forever." For I will restore this country as of old, says the LORD.

Jeremiah 33:10–11

King Hezekiah and the princes then commanded the Levites to sing the praises of the LORD in the words of David and of Asaph the seer. They sang praises till their joy was full, then fell down and prostrated themselves.

2 Chronicles 29:30

Happy the people who know you, LORD,
who walk in the radiance of your face.

Psalm 89:16

The LORD, your God, is in your midst,
 a mighty savior;
He will rejoice over you with gladness,
 and renew you in his love,
He will sing joyfully because of you.

Zephaniah 3:17

But let those who favor my just cause
 shout for joy and be glad.
May they ever say, "Exalted be the LORD
 who delights in the peace of his loyal servant."
Then my tongue shall recount your justice,
 declare your praise, all the day long.

Psalm 35:27–28

LORD, incline your heavens and come;
 touch the mountains and make them smoke.

Psalm 144:5

God Teaches a Woman How to . . .
Trust Him Completely ✍

Beloved, do not trust every spirit but test the spirits to see whether they belong to God, because many false prophets have gone out into the world.

1 John 4:1

The LORD is your guardian;
  the LORD is your shade
  at your right hand.
The LORD will guard you from all evil,
  will always guard your life.
The LORD will guard your coming and going
  both now and forever.

Psalm 121:5, 7–8

Such confidence we have through Christ toward God. Not that of ourselves we are qualified to take credit for anything as coming from us; rather, our qualification comes from God.

2 Corinthians 3:4–5

When I caught sight of him, I fell down at his feet as though dead. He touched me with his right hand and said, "Do not be afraid. I am the first and the last."

Revelation 1:17–18

The LORD is my shepherd;
　　there is nothing I lack.
In green pastures you let me graze;
　　to safe waters you lead me;
　　you restore my strength.
You guide me along the right path
　　for the sake of your name.
Even when I walk through a dark valley,
　　I fear no harm for you are at my side;
　　your rod and staff give me courage.

Psalm 23:1b–4

My help comes from the LORD,
　　the maker of heaven and earth.
God will not allow your foot to slip;
　　your guardian does not sleep.

Psalm 121:2–3

Say to the LORD, "My refuge and fortress,
　　my God in whom I trust."
God will rescue you from the fowler's snare,
　　from the destroying plague,
Will shelter you with pinions,
　　spread wings that you may take refuge;
　　God's faithfulness is a protecting shield.

Psalm 91:2–4

God Teaches a Woman How to . . .
Hold On to Faith 🖎

So there are three that testify, the Spirit, the water, and the blood, and the three are of one accord.

1 John 5:7–8

Let us hold unwaveringly to our confession that gives us hope, for he who made the promise is trustworthy.

Hebrews 10:23

I command you: be firm and steadfast! Do not fear nor be dismayed, for the LORD, your God, is with you wherever you go.

Joshua 1:9

For nothing will be impossible for God.

Luke 1:37

Beloved, although I was making every effort to write to you about our common salvation, I now feel a need to write to encourage you to contend for the faith that was once for all handed down to the holy ones.

Jude 3

For we walk by faith, not by sight.

2 Corinthians 5:7

So stand fast with your loins girded in truth, clothed with righteousness as a breasteplate, and your feet shod in readiness for the gospel of peace. In all circumstances, hold faith as a shield, to quench all [the] flaming arrows of the evil one.

Ephesians 6:14–16

But you, beloved, build yourselves up in your most holy faith; pray in the holy Spirit. Keep yourselves in the love of God and wait for the mercy of our Lord Jesus Christ that leads to eternal life.

Jude 20–21

Therefore, my beloved brothers, be firm, steadfast, always fully devoted to the work of the Lord, knowing that in the Lord your labor is not in vain.

1 Corinthians 15:58

To the one who is able to keep you from stumbling…be glory, majesty, power, and authority from ages past, now, and for ages to come. Amen.

Jude 24a, 25b

God Teaches a Woman How to . . .
Have Joy in Him ✍

I tell you, in just the same way there will be more joy in heaven over one sinner who repents than over ninety-nine righteous people who have no need of repentance.

Luke 15:7

This is the day the LORD has made;
let us rejoice in it and be glad.

Psalm 118:24

I have told you this so that my joy may be in you and your joy may be complete. This is my commandment: love one another as I love you.

John 15:11–12

A clean heart create for me, God;
renew in me a steadfast spirit.
Do not drive me from your presence,
nor take from me your holy spirit.
Restore my joy in your salvation;
sustain in me a willing spirit.

Psalm 51:12–14

Let us greet him with a song of praise,
  joyfully sing out our psalms.

Psalm 95:2

For your love is better than life;
  my lips offer you worship!

I will bless you as long as I live;
  I will lift up my hands, calling on your name.
My soul shall savor the rich banquet of praise,
  with joyous lips my mouth shall honor you!

Psalm 63:4–6

  For the kingdom of God is not a matter of food
and drink, but of righteousness, peace, and joy in
the holy Spirit.

Romans 14:17

A glad heart lights up the face,
  but by mental anguish the spirit is broken.

Proverbs 15:13

Fill us at daybreak with your love,
  that all our days we may sing for joy.

Psalm 90:14

God Teaches a Woman How to . . .
Center Her Life in Him ✍

Yes, all shall be put to shame and disgrace
  who vent their anger against you;
Those shall perish and come to nought
  who offer resistance.
You shall seek out, but shall not find,
  those who strive against you;
They shall be as nothing at all
  who do battle with you.

For I am the LORD, your God,
  who grasp your right hand;
It is I who say to you, "Fear not,
  I will help you."

Isaiah 41:11–13

    Let the word of Christ dwell in you richly, as in all wisdom you teach and admonish one another, singing psalms, hymns, and spiritual songs with gratitude in your hearts to God.

Colossians 3:16

I sought the LORD, who answered me,
  delivered me from all my fears.

Psalm 34:5

I will sing to the LORD all my life;
  I will sing praise to my God while I live.
May my theme be pleasing to God;
  I will rejoice in the LORD.

Psalm 104:33–34

For the grace of God has appeared, saving all
and training us to reject godless ways and worldly
desires and to live temperately, justly, and devoutly
in this age, as we await the blessed hope, the
appearance of the glory of the great God and of our
savior Jesus Christ.

Titus 2:11–13

Yet I live, no longer I, but Christ lives in me;
insofar as I now live in the flesh, I live by faith in
the Son of God who has loved me and given
himself up for me.

Galatians 2:20

At dawn you will hear my cry;
  at dawn I will plead before you and wait.

Psalm 5:4

God Teaches a Woman How to . . .
Rest in His Protection ✍

The LORD is my light and my salvation;
 whom do I fear?
The LORD is my life's refuge;
 of whom am I afraid?
When evildoers come at me
 to devour my flesh,
These my enemies and foes
 themselves stumble and fall.
Though an army encamp against me,
 my heart does not fear;
Though war be waged against me,
 even then do I trust.

One thing I ask of the LORD;
 this I seek:
To dwell in the LORD'S house
 all the days of my life,
To gaze on the LORD'S beauty,
 to visit his temple.
For God will hide me in his shelter
 in time of trouble,
Will conceal me in the cover of his tent;
 and set me high upon a rock.

Psalm 27:1–5

But he who obeys me dwells in security,
in peace, without fear of harm.

Proverbs 1:33

With full voice I cry to the LORD;
with full voice I beseech the LORD.
Before God I pour out my complaint,
lay bare my distress.

Psalm 142:2–3

The LORD is your guardian;
the LORD is your shade
at your right hand.
By day the sun cannot harm you,
nor the moon by night.
The LORD will guard you from all evil,
will always guard your life.
The LORD will guard your coming and going
both now and forever.

Psalm 121:5–8

No weapon fashioned against you shall prevail;
every tongue you shall prove false
that launches an accusation against you.
This is the lot of the servants of the LORD,
their vindication from me, says the LORD.

Isaiah 54:17

In peace I shall both lie down and sleep,
    for you alone, LORD, make me secure.

Psalm 4:9

When you pass through the water, I will be with
        you;
    in the rivers you shall not drown.
When you walk through fire, you shall not be
            burned;
    the flames shall not consume you.

Isaiah 43:2

May God send you help from the temple,
    from Zion be your support.

Psalm 20:3

    But the Lord is faithful; he will strengthen you
and guard you from the evil one.

2 Thessalonians 3:3

God Teaches a Woman How to . . .
Obtain His Promises 🐚

And we have this confidence in him, that if we ask anything according to his will, he hears us. And if we know that he hears us in regard to whatever we ask, we know that what we have asked him for is ours.

1 John 5:14–15

"If you really listen to the voice of the LORD, your God," he told them, "and do what is right in his eyes: if you heed his commandments and keep all his precepts, I will not afflict you with any of the diseases with which I afflicted the Egyptians; for I, the LORD, am your healer."

Exodus 15:26

But seek first the kingdom [of God] and his righteousness, and all these things will be given you besides.

Matthew 6:33

We earnestly desire each of you to demonstrate the same eagerness for the fulfillment of hope until the end, so that you may not become sluggish, but imitators of those who, through faith and patience, are inheriting the promises.

Let us hold unwaveringly to our confession that gives us hope, for he who made the promise is trustworthy.

Hebrews 10:23

Through these, he has bestowed on us the precious and very great promises, so that through them you may come to share in the divine nature, after escaping from the corruption that is in the world because of evil desire. For this very reason, make every effort to supplement your faith with virtue, virtue with knowledge, knowledge with self-control, self-control with endurance, endurance with devotion, devotion with mutual affection, mutual affection with love. If these are yours and increase in abundance, they will keep you from being idle or unfruitful in the knowledge of our Lord Jesus Christ.

2 Peter 1:4–8

Faith is the realization of what is hoped for and evidence of things not seen. But without faith it is impossible to please him, for anyone who approaches God must believe that he exists and that he rewards those who seek him. By faith he

[Abraham] received power to generate, even though he was past the normal age—and Sarah herself was sterile—for he thought that the one who had made the promise was trustworthy.

Hebrews 11:1, 6, 11

For nothing will be impossible for God.

Luke 1:37

God Blesses Women When They . . .
Trust in His Power ॐ

In the LORD I take refuge;
  how can you say to me,
  "Flee like a bird to the mountains!
See how the wicked string their bows,
  fit their arrows to the string
  to shoot from the shadows at the upright.
When foundations are being destroyed,
  what can the upright do?"

The LORD is in his holy temple;
  the LORD'S throne is in heaven.
God's eyes keep careful watch;
  they test all peoples.
The LORD tests the good and the bad,
  hates those who love violence,
And rains upon the wicked
  fiery coals and brimstone,
  a scorching wind their allotted cup.
The LORD is just and loves just deeds;
  the upright shall see his face.

Psalm 11:1b–7

Trust God at all times, my people!
  Pour out your hearts to God our refuge!

Psalm 62:9

Like Mount Zion are they
   who trust in the LORD,
   unshakable, forever enduring.
As mountains surround Jerusalem,
   the LORD surrounds his people
   both now and forever.

The scepter of the wicked will not prevail
   in the land given to the just,
Lest the just themselves
   turn their hands to evil.

Do good, LORD, to the good,
   to those who are upright of heart.
But those who turn aside to crooked ways
   may the LORD send down with the wicked.
Peace upon Israel!

Psalm 125:1b–5

You, LORD, give light to my lamp;
   my God brightens the darkness about me.
With you I can rush an armed band,
   with my God to help I can leap a wall.
God's way is unerring;
   the LORD'S promise is tried and true;
   he is a shield for all who trust in him.

Psalm 18:29–31

When I am afraid,
in you I place my trust.
God, I praise your promise;
in you I trust, I do not fear.
What can mere flesh do to me?

Psalm 56:4–5

How many are my foes, LORD!
How many rise against me!
How many say of me,
"God will not save that one."
But you, LORD, are a shield around me;
my glory, you keep my head high.

Whenever I cried out to the LORD,
I was answered from the holy mountain.

Whenever I lay down and slept,
the LORD preserved me to rise again.
I do not fear, then, thousands of people
arrayed against me on every side.

Arise, LORD! Save me, my God!
You will shatter the jaws of all my foes;
you will break the teeth of the wicked.
Safety comes from the LORD!
Your blessing for your people!

Psalm 3:2–9

In you I trust, I do not fear.
What can mere mortals do to me?

I have made vows to you, God;
   with offerings I will fulfill them.

Psalm 56:12–13

Yet you are enthroned as the Holy One;
   you are the glory of Israel.
In you our ancestors trusted;
   they trusted and you rescued them.

Psalm 22:4–5

God will rescue you from the fowler's snare,
   from the destroying plague,
Will shelter you with pinions,
   spread wings that you may take refuge;
   God's faithfulness is a protecting shield.

Psalm 91:3-4

God Blesses Women When They . . .
Praise His Goodness ❧

Let the faithful rejoice in their glory,
    cry out for joy at their banquet,
With the praise of God in their mouths,
    and a two-edged sword in their hands.

Psalm 149:5–6

My heart is steadfast, God,
    my heart is steadfast.
    I will sing and chant praise.
Awake, my soul;
    awake, lyre and harp!
    I will wake the dawn.
I will praise you among the peoples, Lord;
    I will chant your praise among the nations.

Psalm 57:8–10

Give praise with crashing cymbals,
    praise him with sounding cymbals.
Let everything that has breath
    give praise to the LORD!
Hallelujah!

Psalm 150:5–6

For your love is better than life;

my lips offer you worship!
I will bless you as long as I live;
  I will lift up my hands, calling on your name.

Psalm 63:4–5

Praise the LORD, who is so good;
  God's love endures forever;
Praise the God of gods;
  God's love endures forever;
Praise the Lord of lords;
  God's love endures forever;

Who alone has done great wonders,
  God's love endures forever.

Psalm 136:1–4

God, I praise your promise.

Psalm 56:11

I will bless the LORD at all times;
  praise shall be always in my mouth.

Psalm 34:2

Those who offer praise as a sacrifice honor me;
  to the obedient I will show the salvation of God.

Psalm 50:23

God Blesses Women When They . . .
Hope in His Faithfulness ☙

We are afflicted in every way, but not constrained; perplexed, but not driven to despair; persecuted, but not abandoned; struck down, but not destroyed; always carrying about in the body the dying of Jesus, so that the life of Jesus may also be manifested in our body. For we who live are constantly being given up to death for the sake of Jesus, so that the life of Jesus may be manifested in our mortal flesh.

2 Corinthians 4:8–11

For this momentary light affliction is producing for us an eternal weight of glory beyond all comparison, as we look not to what is seen but to what is unseen; for what is seen is transitory, but what is unseen is eternal.

2 Corinthians 4:17–18

Therefore, do not throw away your confidence; it will have great recompense. You need endurance to do the will of God and receive what he has promised.

Hebrews 10:35–36

The favors of the LORD are not exhausted,
   his mercies are not spent;
They are renewed each morning,
   so great is his faithfulness.
My portion is the LORD, says my soul;
   therefore will I hope in him.

Good is the LORD to one who waits for him,
   to the soul that seeks him.

Lamentations 3:22–25

   For we know that if our earthly dwelling, a tent,
should be destroyed, we have a building from God,
a dwelling not made with hands, eternal in heaven.

2 Corinthians 5:1

But I believe I shall enjoy the LORD'S goodness
   in the land of the living.
Wait for the LORD, take courage;
   be stouthearted, wait for the LORD!

Psalm 27:13–14

   This we have as an anchor of the soul, sure and
firm, which reaches into the interior behind the
veil.

Hebrews 6:19

I wait with longing for the LORD,
  my soul waits for his word.
My soul looks for the Lord
  more than sentinels for daybreak.

Psalm 130:5–6

Morning after morning he renders judgment
  unfailingly, at dawn.

Zephaniah 3:5b

Let us hold unwaveringly to our confession that gives us hope, for he who made the promise is trustworthy.

Hebrews 10:23

God Blesses Women When They . . .
Rest in His Peace ᔰ

For God will hide me in his shelter
   in time of trouble,
Will conceal me in the cover of his tent;
   and set me high upon a rock.

Psalm 27:5

Give us aid against the foe;
   worthless is human help.
We will triumph with the help of God,
   who will trample down our foes.

Psalm 60:13–14

All your sons shall be taught by the LORD,
   and great shall be the peace of your children.
In justice shall you be established,
   far from the fear of oppression,
   where destruction cannot come near you.

Isaiah 54:13–14

Come to me, all you who labor and are burdened,
and I will give you rest.

Matthew 11:28

Then the LORD will guide you always

and give you plenty even on the parched land.
He will renew your strength,
    and you shall be like a watered garden,
    like a spring whose water never fails.

Isaiah 58:11

The spirit of the Lord GOD is upon me,
    because the LORD has anointed me;
He has sent me to bring glad tidings to the lowly,
    to heal the brokenhearted,
To proclaim liberty to the captives
    and release to the prisoners.

Isaiah 61:1

Even if my father and mother forsake me,
    the LORD will take me in.

But I believe I shall enjoy the LORD'S goodness
    in the land of the living.
Wait for the LORD, take courage;
    be stouthearted, wait for the LORD!

Psalm 27:10, 13, 14

May your love comfort me
    in accord with your promise to your servant.
Show me compassion that I may live,
    for your teaching is my delight.

Psalm 119:76–77

Let the words of my mouth meet with your favor,
keep the thoughts of my heart before you,
LORD, my rock and my redeemer.

Psalm 19:15

Anxiety in a man's heart depresses it,
but a kindly word makes it glad.

Proverbs 12:25

God Blesses Women When They . . .
Stand Strong in Faith ❧

But you, beloved, build yourselves up in your most holy faith; pray in the holy Spirit. Keep yourselves in the love of God and wait for the mercy of our Lord Jesus Christ that leads to eternal life.

Jude 20–21

Have no anxiety at all, but in everything, by prayer and petition, with thanksgiving, make your requests known to God. Then the peace of God that surpasses all understanding will guard your hearts and minds in Christ Jesus.

Philippians 4:6–7

Therefore, since we have been justified by faith, we have peace with God through our Lord Jesus Christ, through whom we have gained access [by faith] to this grace in which we stand, and we boast in hope of the glory of God.

Romans 5:1–2

But the Lord is faithful; he will strengthen you and guard you from the evil one.

2 Thessalonians 3:3

My soul, be at rest in God alone,
  from whom comes my hope.
God alone is my rock and my salvation,
  my secure height; I shall not fall.
My safety and glory are with God,
  my strong rock and refuge.

Psalm 62:6–8

But without faith it is impossible to please him,
for anyone who approaches God must believe that
he exists and that he rewards those who seek him.

Hebrews 11:6

And just as Moses lifted up the serpent in the
desert, so must the Son of Man be lifted up, so that
everyone who believes in him may have eternal
life.

John 3:14–15

Faith is the realization of what is hoped for and
evidence of things not seen. Because of it the
ancients were well attested. By faith we understand
that the universe was ordered by the word of God,
so that what is visible came into being through the
invisible.

Hebrews 11:1–3

God Blesses Women When They. . .
Claim His Victory ✍

And put a new song in my mouth,
 a hymn to our God.
Many shall look on in awe
 and they shall trust in the LORD.

Psalm 40:4

The LORD is close to the brokenhearted,
 saves those whose spirit is crushed.
Many are the troubles of the just,
 but the LORD delivers from them all.

Psalm 34:19–20

The Spirit itself bears witness with our spirit that we are children of God, and if children, then heirs, heirs of God and joint heirs with Christ, if only we suffer with him so that we may also be glorified with him.

I consider that the sufferings of this present time are as nothing compared with the glory to be revealed for us.

Romans 8:16–18

Everything that the Father gives me will come to me, and I will not reject anyone who comes to me.

John 6:37

The earth is the LORD'S and all it holds,
  the world and those who live there.
For God founded it on the seas,
  established it over the rivers.

Who may go up the mountain of the LORD?
  Who can stand in his holy place?
 "The clean of hand and pure of heart,
  who are not devoted to idols,
  who have not sworn falsely.
They will receive blessings from the LORD,
  and justice from their saving God.
Such are the people that love the LORD,
  that seek the face of the God of Jacob."

Lift up your heads, O gates;
  rise up, you ancient portals,
  that the king of glory may enter.
Who is this king of glory?
  The LORD, a mighty warrior,
  the LORD, mighty in battle.
Lift up your heads, O gates;
  rise up, you ancient portals,
  that the king of glory may enter.
Who is this king of glory?
  The LORD of hosts is the king of glory.

Psalm 24:1b–10

Great is the LORD and highly praised
   in the city of our God:
The holy mountain.

Psalm 48:1

The LORD is your guardian;
   the LORD is your shade
   at your right hand.
By day the sun cannot harm you,
   nor the moon by night.
The LORD will guard you from all evil,
   will always guard your life.
The LORD will guard your coming and going
   both now and forever.

Psalm 121:5–8

God is king over all the earth;
   sing hymns of praise.
God rules over the nations;
   God sits upon his holy throne.
The princes of the peoples assemble
   with the people of the God of Abraham.
For the rulers of the earth belong to God,
   who is enthroned on high.

Psalm 47:8–10

God Comforts Women as They Learn to . . .
Handle Spiritual Trials ❧

But do not ignore this one fact, beloved, that with the Lord one day is like a thousand years and a thousand years like one day. The Lord does not delay his promise, as some regard "delay," but he is patient with you, not wishing that any should perish but that all should come to repentance.

2 Peter 3:8–9

Cast your care upon the LORD,
    who will give you support.
God will never allow
    the righteous to stumble.

Psalm 55:23

Blessed is the man who perseveres in temptation, for when he has been proved he will receive the crown of life that he promised to those who love him.

For if anyone is a hearer of the word and not a doer, he is like a man who looks at his own face in a mirror. He sees himself, then goes off and promptly forgets what he looked like.

James 1:12, 23–24

Yet he knows my way;
 if he proved me, I should come forth as gold.
My foot has always walked in his steps;
 his way I have kept and have not turned aside.

Job 23:10–11

Why are you downcast, my soul?
 Why do you groan within me?
Wait for God, whom I shall praise again,
 my savior and my God.

Psalm 43:5

Beloved, do not be surprised that a trial by fire is occurring among you, as if something strange were happening to you. But rejoice to the extent that you share in the sufferings of Christ, so that when his glory is revealed you may also rejoice exultantly. But whoever is made to suffer as a Christian should not be ashamed but glorify God because of the name.

1 Peter 4:12–13, 16

If you obey the commandments of the LORD, your God, which I enjoin on you today, loving him, and walking in his ways, and keeping his commandments, statutes and decrees, you will live and grow numerous, and the LORD, your God, will bless you in the land you are entering to occupy.

Deuteronomy 30:16

Answer me, LORD, in your generous love;
  in your great mercy turn to me.
Do not hide your face from your servant;
  in my distress hasten to answer me.
Come and ransom my life;
  because of my enemies redeem me.

Psalm 69:17–19

He who conceals his sins prospers not,
  but he who confesses and forsakes them obtains
      mercy.

Proverbs 28:13

Happy those who observe God's decrees,
  who seek the LORD with all their heart.

Psalm 119:2

Be doers of the word and not hearers only, deluding yourselves.

James 1:22

God Comforts Women as They Learn to . . .
Confront Serious Illness ❧

Heal me, LORD, that I may be healed;
　save me, that I may be saved,
　for it is you whom I praise.

Jeremiah 17:14

I conclude: "My sorrow is this,
　the right hand of the Most High has left us."

I will remember the deeds of the LORD;
　yes, your wonders of old I will remember.
I will recite all your works;
　your exploits I will tell.
Your way, O God, is holy;
　what god is as great as our God?
You alone are the God who did wonders;
　among the peoples you revealed your might.

Psalm 77:11–15

But God will redeem my life,
　will take me from the power of Sheol.

Psalm 49:16

Even when I walk through a dark valley,
　I fear no harm for you are at my side;

your rod and staff give me courage.

Psalm 23:4

For we know that if our earthly dwelling, a tent, should be destroyed, we have a building from God, a dwelling not made with hands, eternal in heaven.

2 Corinthians 5:1

Praise the LORD, my soul;
  I shall praise the LORD all my life,
  sing praise to my God while I live.

Psalm 146:2

Before I was afflicted I went astray,
  but now I hold to your promise.
You are good and do what is good;
  teach me your laws.

Psalm 119:67–68

God Comforts Women as They Learn to . . .
Handle Financial Problems ✍

And the Lord replied, "Who, then, is the faithful and prudent steward whom the master will put in charge of his servants to distribute [the] food allowance at the proper time? Blessed is that servant whom his master on arrival finds doing so. Truly, I say to you, he will put him in charge of all his property.

Luke 12:42–44

For the peace of Jerusalem pray:
"May those who love you prosper!"

Psalm 122:6

He fasted for forty days and forty nights, and afterwards he was hungry. The tempter approached and said to him, "If you are the Son of God, command that these stones become loaves of bread." He said in reply, "It is written:
'One does not live by bread alone,
but by every word that comes forth
from the mouth of God.'"

Matthew 4:2–4

My God will fully supply whatever you need, in accord with his glorious riches in Christ Jesus.

Philippians 4:19

Listen, my beloved brothers. Did not God choose those who are poor in the world to be rich in faith and heirs of the kingdom that he promised to those who love him?

James 2:5

He who trusts in his riches will fall,
    but like green leaves the just flourish.

Proverbs 11:28

He said to [his] disciples, "Therefore I tell you, do not worry about your life and what you will eat, or about your body and what you will wear. For life is more than food and the body more than clothing. Notice the ravens: they do not sow or reap; they have neither storehouse nor barn, yet God feeds them. How much more important are you than birds!"

Luke 12:22–24

Poverty and shame befall the man
    who disregards correction,
    but he who heeds reproof is honored.

Proverbs 13:18

God Comforts Women as They Learn to . . .
Face the Years Ahead ॐ

At present we see indistinctly, as in a mirror, but then face to face. At present I know partially; then I shall know fully, as I am fully known.

1 Corinthians 13:12

The just shall flourish like the palm tree,
    shall grow like a cedar of Lebanon.
Planted in the house of the LORD,
    they shall flourish in the courts of our God.
They shall bear fruit even in old age,
    always vigorous and sturdy,
As they proclaim: "The LORD is just;
    our rock, in whom there is no wrong."

Psalm 92:13–16

None of us lives for oneself, and no one dies for oneself. For if we live, we live for the Lord, and if we die, we die for the Lord; so then, whether we live or die, we are the Lord's.

Romans 14:7–8

The fear of the LORD prolongs life,
    but the years of the wicked are brief.

Proverbs 10:27

Seventy is the sum of our years,
  or eighty, if we are strong;
Most of them are sorrow and toil;
  they pass quickly, we are all but gone.
Teach us to count our days aright,
  that we may gain wisdom of heart.
Fill us at daybreak with your love,
  that all our days we may sing for joy.

Psalm 90:10, 12, 14

Older men should be temperate, dignified, self-controlled, sound in faith, love, and endurance. Similarly, older women should be reverent in their behavior, not slanderers, not addicted to drink, teaching what is good, so that they may train younger women to love their husbands and children.

Titus 2:2–4

But I trust in you, LORD;
  I say, "You are my God."
My times are in your hands;
  rescue me from my enemies,
  from the hands of my pursuers.

Psalm 31:15–16

But as for me, I know that my Vindicator lives,
  and that he will at last stand forth upon the dust;
And from my flesh I shall see God;
  my inmost being is consumed with longing.

Job 19:25–26

God Comforts Women as They Learn to . . .
Call on God's Divine Protection ❧

In peace I shall both lie down and sleep,
   for you alone, LORD, make me secure.

Psalm 4:9

The angel of the LORD, who encamps
   with them,
delivers all who fear God.

Psalm 34:8

You who dwell in the shelter of the Most High,
   who abide in the shadow of the Almighty,
Say to the LORD, "My refuge and fortress,
   my God in whom I trust."

Psalm 91:1–2

Those in the west shall fear the name of the LORD,
   and those in the east, his glory;
For it shall come like a pent-up river
   which the breath of the LORD drives on.

Isaiah 59:19

The LORD is my light and my salvation;
   whom do I fear?
The LORD is my life's refuge;

of whom am I afraid?

For God will hide me in his shelter
　in time of trouble,
Will conceal me in the cover of his tent;
　and set me high upon a rock.

Psalm 27:1b, 5

　　Are not two sparrows sold for a small coin? Yet not one of them falls to the ground without your Father's knowledge. Even all the hairs of your head are counted. So do not be afraid; you are worth more than many sparrows.

Matthew 10:29–31

He spread out the primeval tent;
　he extended the ancient canopy.
He drove the enemy out of your way
　and the Amorite he destroyed.

Deuteronomy 33:27

But he who obeys me dwells in security,
　in peace, without fear of harm.

Proverbs 1:33

God Comforts Women as They Learn to . . .
Be Content ❧

Though the mountains leave their place
  and the hills be shaken,
My love shall never leave you
  nor my covenant of peace be shaken,
  says the LORD, who has mercy on you.

All your sons shall be taught by the LORD,
  and great shall be the peace of your children.
No weapon fashioned against you shall prevail;
  every tongue you shall prove false
  that launches an accusation against you.
This is the lot of the servants of the LORD,
  their vindication from me, says the LORD.

Isaiah 54:10, 13, 17

    Not that I say this because of need, for I have learned, in whatever situation I find myself, to be self-sufficient. I know indeed how to live in humble circumstances; I know also how to live with abundance. In every circumstance and in all things I have learned the secret of being well fed and of going hungry, of living in abundance and of being in need.

Philippians 4:11–12

Hence, now there is no condemnation for those who are in Christ Jesus. For the law of the spirit of life in Christ Jesus has freed you from the law of sin and death. For those who live according to the flesh are concerned with the things of the flesh, but those who live according to the spirit with the things of the spirit. The concern of the flesh is death, but the concern of the spirit is life and peace.

Romans 8:1–2, 5–6

Indeed, religion with contentment is a great gain. For we brought nothing into the world, just as we shall not be able to take anything out of it. If we have food and clothing, we shall be content with that.

1 Timothy 6:6–8

The LORD is my shepherd;
there is nothing I lack.

Psalm 23:1

Then the LORD will guide you always
and give you plenty even on the parched land.
He will renew your strength,
and you shall be like a watered garden,
like a spring whose water never fails.

Isaiah 58:11

Not that of ourselves we are qualified to take credit for anything as coming from us; rather, our qualification comes from God.

2 Corinthians 3:5

The LORD is your guardian;
  the LORD is your shade
  at your right hand.
The LORD will guard your coming and going
  both now and forever.

Psalm 121:5, 8

But as it is written:
  "What eye has not seen, and ear has not heard,
  and what has not entered the human heart,
  what God has prepared for those who
    love him."

1 Corinthians 2:9

And you share in this fullness in him, who is the head of every principality and power.

Colossians 2:10

God Gives Freely to Women . . .
Hope for Eternal Life ❧

Sing to the LORD with thanksgiving;
   with the lyre celebrate our God,
Who covers the heavens with clouds,
   provides rain for the earth,
   makes grass sprout on the mountains,
Who gives animals their food
   and ravens what they cry for.
God takes no delight in the strength of horses,
   no pleasure in the runner's stride.
Rather the LORD takes pleasure in the devout,
   those who await his faithful care.

Glorify the LORD, Jerusalem;
   Zion, offer praise to your God,
Who has strengthened the bars of your gates,
   blessed your children within you.

Psalm 147:7–13

    If then you were raised with Christ, seek what is above, where Christ is seated at the right hand of God. Think of what is above, not of what is on earth. For you have died, and your life is hidden with Christ in God. When Christ your life appears, then you too will appear with him in glory.

Colossians 3:1–4

But since we are of the day, let us be sober, putting on the breastplate of faith and love and the helmet that is hope for salvation. For God did not destine us for wrath, but to gain salvation through our Lord Jesus Christ, who died for us, so that whether we are awake or asleep we may live together with him. Therefore, encourage one another and build one another up, as indeed you do.

1 Thessalonians 5:8–11

But God, who is rich in mercy, because of the great love he had for us, even when we were dead in our transgressions, brought us to life with Christ (by grace you have been saved), raised us up with him, and seated us with him in the heavens in Christ Jesus, that in the ages to come he might show the immeasurable riches of his grace in his kindness to us in Christ Jesus.

Ephesians 2:4–7

I have competed well; I have finished the race; I have kept the faith. From now on the crown of righteousness awaits me, which the Lord, the just judge, will award to me on that day, and not only to me, but to all who have longed for his appearance.

2 Timothy 4:7–8

[Yet] who know that a person is not justified by works of the law but through faith in Jesus Christ, even we have believed in Christ Jesus that we may be justified by faith in Christ and not by works of the law, because by works of the law no one will be justified…yet I live, no longer I, but Christ lives in me; insofar as I now live in the flesh, I live by faith in the Son of God who has loved me and given himself up for me.

Galatians 2:16, 20

Those who are led by the Spirit of God are children of God. For you did not receive a spirit of slavery to fall back into fear, but you received a spirit of adoption, through which we cry, "*Abba, Father!*" The Spirit itself bears witness with our spirit that we are children of God, and if children, then heirs, heirs of God and joint heirs with Christ, if only we suffer with him so that we may also be glorified with him.

I consider that the sufferings of this present time are as nothing compared with the glory to be revealed for us. For in hope we were saved. Now hope that sees for itself is not hope. For who hopes for what one sees? But if we hope for what we do not see, we wait with endurance.

Romans 8:14–18, 24–25

Blessed be the God and Father of our Lord Jesus Christ, who in his great mercy gave us a new birth to a living hope through the resurrection of Jesus Christ from the dead, to an inheritance that is imperishable, undefiled, and unfading, kept in heaven for you who by the power of God are safeguarded through faith, to a salvation that is ready to be revealed in the final time. In this you rejoice, although now for a little while you may have to suffer through various trials, so that the genuineness of your faith, more precious than gold that is perishable even though tested by fire, may prove to be for praise, glory, and honor at the revelation of Jesus Christ. Although you have not seen him you love him; even though you do not see him now yet believe in him, you rejoice with an indescribable and glorious joy, as you attain the goal of [your] faith, the salvation of your souls.

1 Peter 1:3–9

For we have heard of your faith in Christ Jesus, and the love that you have for all the holy ones because of the hope reserved for you in heaven. Of this you have already heard through the word of truth, the gospel, that has come to you. Just as in the whole world it is bearing fruit and growing, so also among you, from the day you heard it and came to know the grace of God in truth.

Colossians 1:4–6

God Gives Freely to Women . . .
Wisdom for Daily Living 🐦

My son, to my wisdom be attentive,
  to my knowledge incline your ear,
That discretion may watch over you,
  and understanding may guard you.

Proverbs 5:1–2

The fear of the LORD is the beginning of wisdom;
  prudent are all who live by it.
  Your praise endures forever.

Psalm 111:10

Seventy is the sum of our years,
  or eighty, if we are strong;
Most of them are sorrow and toil;
  they pass quickly, we are all but gone.
Who comprehends your terrible anger?
  Your wrath matches the fear it inspires.
Teach us to count our days aright,
  that we may gain wisdom of heart.

Psalm 90:10–12

How much better to acquire wisdom
    than gold!
  To acquire understanding is more

desirable than silver.

Proverbs 16:16

The wise man is cautious and shuns evil;
  the fool is reckless and sure of himself.

Proverbs 14:16

Happy the man who finds wisdom,
  the man who gains understanding!
For her profit is better than profit in silver,
  and better than gold is her revenue;
She is more precious than corals,
  and none of your choice possessions
  can compare with her.

Long life is in her right hand,
  in her left are riches and honor;
Her ways are pleasant ways,
  and all her paths are peace;
She is a tree of life to those who grasp her,
  and he is happy who holds her fast.

The LORD by wisdom founded the earth,
  established the heavens by understanding;
By his knowledge the depths break open,
  and the clouds drop down dew.
My son, let not these slip out of your sight:
  keep advice and counsel in view;

So will they be life to your soul,
  and an adornment for your neck.

Proverbs 3:13–22

But if any of you lacks wisdom, he should ask God who gives to all generously and ungrudgingly, and he will be given it. But he should ask in faith, not doubting, for the one who doubts is like a wave of the sea that is driven and tossed about by the wind.

James 1:5–6

"Get wisdom, get understanding!
  Do not forget or turn aside from the words I utter.
Forsake her not, and she will preserve you;
  love her, and she will safeguard you;
The beginning of wisdom is: get wisdom;
  at the cost of all you have, get understanding.
Extol her, and she will exalt you;
  she will bring you honors if you embrace her;
She will put on your head a graceful diadem;
  a glorious crown will she bestow on you."

Hear, my son, and receive my words,
  and the years of your life shall be many.
On the way of wisdom I direct you,
  I lead you on straightforward paths.

Proverbs 4:5–11

My son, keep my words,
  and treasure my commands.
Keep my commands and live,
  my teaching as the apple of your eye;
Bind them on your fingers,
  write them on the tablet of your heart.
Say to Wisdom, "You are my sister!"
  call Understanding, "Friend!"
That they may keep you from another's wife,
  from the adulteress with her smooth words.

Proverbs 7:1–5

The beginning of wisdom is the fear of the LORD,
  and knowledge of the Holy One is understanding.
"For by me your days will be multiplied
  and the years of your life increased."
If you are wise, it is to your own advantage;
  and if you are arrogant, you alone shall bear it.

Proverbs 9:10–12

But the wisdom from above is first of all pure, then
peaceable, gentle, compliant, full of mercy and
good fruits, without inconstancy or insincerity.

James 3:17

God Gives Freely to Women . . .
Victory Over Sin

So whoever is in Christ is a new creation: the old things have passed away; behold, new things have come. And all this is from God, who has reconciled us to himself through Christ and given us the ministry of reconciliation, namely, God was reconciling the world to himself in Christ, not counting their trespasses against them and entrusting to us the message of reconciliation. So we are ambassadors for Christ, as if God were appealing through us. We implore you on behalf of Christ, be reconciled to God. For our sake he made him to be sin who did not know sin, so that we might become the righteousness of God in him.

2 Corinthians 5:17–21

God, you know my folly;
  my faults are not hidden from you.

Psalm 69:6

For all who depend on works of the law are under a curse; for it is written, "Cursed be everyone who does not persevere in doing all the things written in the book of the law." And that no one is justified before God by the law is clear, for

"the one who is righteous by faith will live."
Galatians 3:10–11

For freedom Christ set us free; so stand firm and do not submit again to the yoke of slavery.
Galatians 5:1

Now this is the message that we have heard from him and proclaim to you: God is light, and in him there is no darkness at all. If we say, "We have fellowship with him," while we continue to walk in darkness, we lie and do not act in truth. But if we walk in the light as he is in the light, then we have fellowship with one another, and the blood of his Son Jesus cleanses us from all sin. If we say, "We are without sin," we deceive ourselves, and the truth is not in us. If we acknowledge our sins, he is faithful and just and will forgive our sins and cleanse us from every wrongdoing. If we say, "We have not sinned," we make him a liar, and his word is not in us.

1 John 1:5–10

Yet I live, no longer I, but Christ lives in me.
Galatians 2:20a

A clean heart create for me, God;
  renew in me a steadfast spirit.

Psalm 51:12

Wash yourselves clean!
Put away your misdeeds from before my eyes;
  cease doing evil; learn to do good.
Make justice your aim: redress the wronged,
  hear the orphan's plea, defend the widow.

Come now, let us set things right,
  says the LORD:
Though your sins be like scarlet,
  they may become white as snow;
Though they be crimson red,
  they may become white as wool.
If you are willing, and obey,
  you shall eat the good things of the land.

Isaiah 1:16–19

You know that he was revealed to take away sins, and in him there is no sin. No one who remains in him sins; no one who sins has seen him or known him. Children, let no one deceive you. The person who acts in righteousness is righteous, just as he is righteous.

1 John 3:5–7

On the way of wisdom I direct you,
  I lead you on straightforward paths.

Proverbs 4:11

Therefore, since we have this ministry through the mercy shown us, we are not discouraged. Rather, we have renounced shameful, hidden things; not acting deceitfully or falsifying the word of God, but by the open declaration of the truth we commend ourselves to everyone's conscience in the sight of God. And even though our gospel is veiled, it is veiled for those who are perishing, in whose case the god of this age has blinded the minds of the unbelievers, so that they may not see the light of the gospel of the glory of Christ, who is the image of God. For we do not preach ourselves but Jesus Christ as Lord, and ourselves as your slaves for the sake of Jesus. For God who said, "Let light shine out of darkness," has shone in our hearts to bring to light the knowledge of the glory of God on the face of [Jesus] Christ.

2 Corinthians 4:1–6

God Gives Freely to Women . . .
Comfort in Troubled Times ✒

The LORD rebuilds Jerusalem,
   gathers the dispersed of Israel,
Heals the brokenhearted,
   binds up their wounds,
Great is our Lord, vast in power,
   with wisdom beyond measure.
The LORD sustains the poor,
   but casts the wicked to the ground.

Who has strengthened the bars of your gates,
   blessed your children within you,
Brought peace to your borders,
   and filled you with finest wheat.

Psalm 147:2–3, 5–6, 13–14

   Peace I leave with you; my peace I give to you.
Not as the world gives do I give it to you. Do not let
your hearts be troubled or afraid.

John 14:27

Look upon me, have pity on me,
   for I am alone and afflicted.
Relieve the troubles of my heart;
   bring me out of my distress.

Put an end to my affliction and suffering;
    take away all my sins.

Psalm 25:16–18

Cast all your worries upon him because he cares for you.

Be sober and vigilant. Your opponent the devil is prowling around like a roaring lion looking for [someone] to devour. Resist him, steadfast in faith, knowing that your fellow believers throughout the world undergo the same sufferings. The God of all grace who called you to his eternal glory through Christ [Jesus] will himself restore, confirm, strengthen, and establish you after you have suffered a little. To him be dominion forever. Amen.

1 Peter 5:7–11

Useless is the horse for safety;
    its great strength, no sure escape.
But the LORD's eyes are upon the reverent,
    upon those who hope for his gracious help,
Delivering them from death,
    keeping them alive in times of famine.

Our soul waits for the LORD,
    who is our help and shield.
For in God our hearts rejoice;
    in your holy name we trust.

May your kindness, LORD, be upon us;
  we have put our hope in you.

Psalm 33:17–22

None of us lives for oneself, and no one dies for oneself.

Romans 14:7

I will bless the LORD at all times;
  praise shall be always in my mouth.
My soul will glory in the LORD
  that the poor may hear and be glad.
Magnify the LORD with me;
  let us exalt his name together.

I sought the LORD, who answered me,
  delivered me from all my fears.
Look to God that you may be radiant with joy
  and your faces may not blush for shame.
In my misfortune I called,
  the LORD heard and saved me from all distress.
The angel of the LORD, who encamps with them,
  delivers all who fear God.
Learn to savor how good the LORD is;
  happy are those who take refuge in him.

Psalm 34:2–9

God Gives Freely to Women . . .
Power to Defeat Fear ৵৯

No, in all these things we conquer
overwhelmingly through him who loved us. For I
am convinced that neither death, nor life, nor
angels, nor principalities, nor present things, nor
future things, nor powers, nor height, nor depth,
nor any other creature will be able to separate us
from the love of God in Christ Jesus our Lord.

Romans 8:37–39

You, LORD, give light to my lamp;
  my God brightens the darkness about me.
With you I can rush an armed band,
  with my God to help I can leap a wall.
God's way is unerring;
  the LORD'S promise is tried and true;
  he is a shield for all who trust in him.

Psalm 18:29–31

Jesus spoke to them again, saying, "I am the
light of the world. Whoever follows me will not
walk in darkness, but will have the light of life."

John 8:12

The LORD is my light and my salvation;

whom do I fear?
The LORD is my life's refuge;
  of whom am I afraid?
When evildoers come at me
  to devour my flesh,
These my enemies and foes
  themselves stumble and fall.
Though an army encamp against me,
  my heart does not fear;
Though war be waged against me,
  even then do I trust.

One thing I ask of the LORD;
  this I seek:
To dwell in the LORD'S house
  all the days of my life,
To gaze on the LORD'S beauty,
  to visit his temple.
For God will hide me in his shelter
  in time of trouble,
Will conceal me in the cover of his tent;
  and set me high upon a rock.
Even now my head is held high
  above my enemies on every side!
I will offer in his tent
  sacrifices with shouts of joy;
    I will sing and chant praise to the LORD.

Hear my voice, LORD, when I call;
   have mercy on me and answer me.

Psalm 27:1b–7

Be not afraid of sudden terror,
   of the ruin of the wicked when it comes;
For the LORD will be your confidence,
   and will keep your foot from the snare.

Proverbs 3:25–26

Find your delight in the LORD
   who will give you your heart's desire.

Commit your way to the LORD;
   trust that God will act
And make your integrity shine like the dawn,
   your vindication like noonday.

Psalm 37:4–6

He said:
I love you, LORD, my strength,
   LORD, my rock, my fortress, my deliverer,
My God, my rock of refuge,
   my shield, my saving horn, my stronghold!
Praised be the LORD, I exclaim!
   I have been delivered from my enemies.

Psalm 18:2–4

It is the LORD, your God, who will cross before you; he will destroy these nations before you, that you may supplant them. [It is Joshua who will cross before you, as the LORD promised.]

It is the LORD who marches before you; he will be with you and will never fail you or forsake you. So do not fear or be dismayed.

Deuteronomy 31:3, 8

While from behind, a voice shall sound in your
    ears:
  "This is the way; walk in it,"
when you would turn to the right or to the left.

Isaiah 30:21

So let us confidently approach the throne of grace to receive mercy and to find grace for timely help.

Hebrews 4:16

God Gives Freely to Women . . .
Courage to Be Women
of Integrity ✍

Happy those who do not follow
    the counsel of the wicked,
Nor go the way of sinners,
    nor sit in company with scoffers.
Rather, the law of the LORD is their joy;
    God's law they study day and night.
They are like a tree
    planted near streams of water,
    that yields its fruit in season;
Its leaves never wither;
    whatever they do prospers.

But not the wicked!
    They are like chaff driven by the wind.
Therefore the wicked will not survive judgment,
    nor will sinners in the assembly of the just.
The LORD watches over the way of the just,
    but the way of the wicked leads to ruin.

Psalm 1:1–6

O LORD, judge of the nations.
Grant me justice, LORD, for I am blameless,
    free of any guilt.

Psalm 7:9

When a man walks in integrity and justice,
  happy are his children after him!

Proverbs 20:7

I follow the way of integrity;
  when will you come to me?
I act with integrity of heart
  within my royal court.
I do not allow into my presence
  anyone who speaks perversely.
Whoever acts shamefully I hate;
  no such person can be my friend.
I shun the devious of heart;
  the wicked I do not tolerate.
Whoever slanders another in secret
  I reduce to silence.
Haughty eyes and arrogant hearts
  I cannot endure.

I look to the faithful of the land;
  they alone can be my companions.
Those who follow the way of integrity,
  they alone can enter my service.
No one who practices deceit
  can hold a post in my court.
No one who speaks falsely
  can be among my advisors.
Each morning I clear the wicked from the land,

and rid the LORD's city of all evildoers.

Psalm 101:2–8

He tells the truth who states what he is sure of,
  but a lying witness speaks deceitfully.

The prating of some men is like sword thrusts,
  but the tongue of the wise is healing.

Truthful lips endure forever,
  the lying tongue, for only a moment.

Proverbs 12:17–19

All goes well for those gracious in lending,
  who conduct their affairs with justice.
They shall never be shaken;
  the just shall be remembered forever.
They shall not fear an ill report;
  their hearts are steadfast, trusting the LORD.

Psalm 112:5–7

O LORD, judge of the nations.
Grant me justice, LORD, for I am blameless,
  free of any guilt.

Psalm 7:9

If I have walked in falsehood
  and my foot has hastened to deceit;

Let God weigh me in the scales of justice;
thus will he know my innocence!

Job 31:5–6

Far be it from me to account you right;
till I die I will not renounce my innocence.
My justice I maintain and I will not relinquish it;
my heart does not reproach me for any of my
days.

Job 27:5–6

Happy those whose way is blameless,
who walk by the teaching of the LORD.
Happy those who observe God's decrees,
who seek the LORD with all their heart.
They do no wrong;
they walk in God's ways.
You have given them the command
to keep your precepts with care.
May my ways be firm
in the observance of your laws!
Then I will not be ashamed
to ponder all your commands.
I will praise you with sincere heart
as I study your just edicts.
I will keep your laws;
do not leave me all alone.

Psalm 119:1–8

God Helps Women to Grow by . . .
Recognizing Evil ❧

Sometimes a way seems right to a man,
   but the end of it leads to death!

Proverbs 14:12

Beware of false prophets, who come to you in sheep's clothing, but underneath are ravenous wolves. By their fruits you will know them. Do people pick grapes from thornbushes, or figs from thistles?

Matthew 7:15–16

This is how you can know the Spirit of God: every spirit that acknowledges Jesus Christ come in the flesh be longs to God, and every spirit that does not acknowledge Jesus does not belong to God. This is the spirit of the antichrist that, as you heard, is to come, but in fact is already in the world.

1 John 4:2–3

Indeed, the spirits of prophets are under the prophets' control, since he is not the God of disorder but of peace.

1 Corinthians 14:32

They claim to know God, but by their deeds they deny him. They are vile and disobedient and unqualified for any good deed.

Titus 1:16

For God did not give us a spirit of cowardice but rather of power and love and self-control.

2 Timothy 1:7

For there have been some intruders, who long ago were designated for this condemnation, godless persons, who pervert the grace of our God into licentiousness and who deny our only Master and Lord, Jesus Christ.

Jude 4

Many deceivers have gone out into the world, those who do not acknowledge Jesus Christ as coming in the flesh; such is the deceitful one and the antichrist. Anyone who is so "progressive" as not to remain in the teaching of the Christ does not have God; whoever remains in the teaching has the Father and the Son. If anyone comes to you and does not bring this doctrine, do not receive him in your house or even greet him; for whoever greets him shares in his evil works.

2 John 7, 9–11

God Helps Women to Grow by . . .
Controlling the Tongue ❧

No foul language should come out of your mouths, but only such as is good for needed edification, that it may impart grace to those who hear.

Ephesians 4:29

So long as I still have life in me
   and the breath of God is in my nostrils,
My lips shall not speak falsehood,
   nor my tongue utter deceit!

Job 27:3–4

For:
   "Whoever would love life
      and see good days
   must keep the tongue from evil
      and the lips from speaking deceit."

1 Peter 3:10

Be not a witness against your neighbor without just cause,
   thus committing folly with your lips.

Proverbs 24:28

He who guards his mouth and his tongue
  keeps himself from trouble.

Proverbs 21:23

A good person out of the store of goodness in
his heart produces good, but an evil person out of
a store of evil produces evil; for from the fullness of
the heart the mouth speaks.

Luke 6:45

A soothing tongue is a tree of life,
  but a perverse one crushes the spirit.

Proverbs 15:4

If anyone thinks he is religious and does not
bridle his tongue but deceives his heart, his religion
is vain.

James 1:26

Those who offer praise as a sacrifice honor me;
  to the obedient I will show the salvation of God.

Psalm 50:23

Set a guard, LORD, before my mouth,
  a gatekeeper at my lips.

Psalm 141:3

God Helps Women to Grow by . . .
Dealing with Lust ✍

So submit yourselves to God. Resist the devil, and he will flee from you.

James 4:7

I say, then: live by the Spirit and you will certainly not gratify the desire of the flesh. For the flesh has desires against the Spirit, and the Spirit against the flesh; these are opposed to each other, so that you may not do what you want.

Galatians 5:16–17

Rather, each person is tempted when he is lured and enticed by his own desire. Then desire conceives and brings forth sin, and when sin reaches maturity it gives birth to death.

Do not be deceived, my beloved brothers.

James 1:14–16

Then the Lord knows how to rescue the devout from trial and to keep the unrighteous under punishment for the day of judgment.

2 Peter 2:9

The avaricious man is perturbed about
    his wealth,
and he knows not when want will come
    upon him.

Proverbs 28:22

The LORD is far from the wicked,
  but the prayer of the just he hears.

Proverbs 15:29

Be sure of this, that no immoral or impure or greedy person, that is, an idolater, has any inheritance in the kingdom of Christ and of God.

So do not be associated with them. For you were once darkness, but now you are light in the Lord. Live as children of light, for light produces every kind of goodness and righteousness and truth. And do not get drunk on wine, in which lies debauchery, but be filled with the Spirit.

Ephesians 5:5, 7–9, 18

That you should put away the old self of your former way of life, corrupted through deceitful desires, and be renewed in the spirit of your minds, and put on the new self, created in God's way in righteousness and holiness of truth...and do not leave room for the devil.

Ephesians 4:22–24, 27

Consequently, you too must think of yourselves as [being] dead to sin and living for God in Christ Jesus.

Therefore, sin must not reign over your mortal bodies so that you obey their desires.

Romans 6:11–12

God Helps Women to Grow by . . .
Overcoming Worldliness &

Do not conform yourselves to this age but be transformed by the renewal of your mind, that you may discern what is the will of God, what is good and pleasing and perfect.

Romans 12:2

Take no part in the fruitless works of darkness; rather expose them.

Ephesians 5:11

Then he said to all, "If anyone wishes to come after me, he must deny himself and take up his cross daily and follow me. For whoever wishes to save his life will lose it, but whoever loses his life for my sake will save it. What profit is there for one to gain the whole world yet lose or forfeit himself?"

Luke 9:23–25

Do not love the world or the things of the world. If anyone loves the world, the love of the Father is not in him. For all that is in the world, sensual lust, enticement for the eyes, and a pretentious life, is not from the Father but is from the world. Yet the world and its enticement are passing away. But whoever does the will of God remains forever.

1 John 2:15–17

Rather, we have renounced shameful, hidden things; not acting deceitfully or falsifying the word of God, but by the open declaration of the truth we commend ourselves to everyone's conscience in the sight of God.

2 Corinthians 4:2

Think of what is above, not of what is on earth.
Stop lying to one another, since you have taken off the old self with its practices and have put on the new self, which is being renewed, for knowledge, in the image of its creator.

Colossians 3:2, 9–10

And training us to reject godless ways and worldly desires and to live temperately, justly, and devoutly in this age, as we await the blessed hope, the appearance of the glory of the great God and of our savior Jesus Christ.

Titus 2:12–13

I have told you this so that you might have peace in me. In the world you will have trouble, but take courage, I have conquered the world.

John 16:33

Then he said to the crowd, "Take care to guard against all greed, for though one may be rich, one's life does not consist of possessions."

Luke 12:15

Do not be yoked with those who are different, with unbelievers. For what partnership do righteousness and lawlessness have? Or what fellowship does light have with darkness?
"Therefore, come forth from them
and be separate," says the Lord,
"and touch nothing unclean;
then I will receive you."

2 Corinthians 6:14, 17

But you are "a chosen race, a royal priesthood, a holy nation, a people of his own."

1 Peter 2:9a

God Helps Women to Grow by . . .
Putting Aside Pride ❧

But it shall not be so among you. Rather, whoever wishes to be great among you shall be your servant; whoever wishes to be first among you shall be your slave.

Matthew 20:26–27

Likewise, you younger members, be subject to the presbyters. And all of you, clothe yourselves with humility in your dealings with one another, for:
  "God opposes the proud
    but bestows favor on the humble."
So humble yourselves under the mighty hand of God, that he may exalt you in due time.

1 Peter 5:5–6

Man's pride causes his humiliation,
  but he who is humble of spirit obtains honor.

Proverbs 29:23

The reward of humility and fear of the LORD
  is riches, honor and life.

Proverbs 22:4

The LORD is on high, but cares for the lowly

and knows the proud from afar.

The Pharisee took up his position and spoke this prayer to himself, "O God, I thank you that I am not like the rest of humanity—greedy, dishonest, adulterous—or even like this tax collector. I fast twice a week, and I pay tithes on my whole income." But the tax collector stood off at a distance and would not even raise his eyes to heaven but beat his breast and prayed, "O God, be merciful to me a sinner." I tell you, the latter went home justified, not the former; for everyone who exalts himself will be humbled, and the one who humbles himself will be exalted.

Luke 18:11–14

"Whoever boasts, should boast in the Lord." For it is not the one who recommends himself who is approved, but the one whom the Lord recommends.

2 Corinthians 10:17–18

Pride goes before disaster,
  and a haughty spirit before a fall.

It is better to be humble with the meek
  than to share plunder with the proud.

He who plans a thing will be successful;
  happy is he who trusts in the LORD!

Proverbs 16:18–20

So submit yourselves to God. Resist the devil, and he will flee from you. Humble yourselves before the Lord and he will exalt you.

James 4:7, 10

Put on then, as God's chosen ones, holy and beloved, heartfelt compassion, kindness, humility, gentleness, and patience.

Colossians 3:12

I, then, a prisoner for the Lord, urge you to live in a manner worthy of the call you have received.

Ephesians 4:1

God Helps Women to Grow by . . .
Rejoicing in the Lord ❧

Let the word of Christ dwell in you richly, as in all wisdom you teach and admonish one another, singing psalms, hymns, and spiritual songs with gratitude in your hearts to God.

Colossians 3:16

He said further: "Go, eat rich foods and drink sweet drinks, and allot portions to those who had nothing prepared; for today is holy to our LORD. Do not be saddened this day, for rejoicing in the LORD must be your strength!"

Nehemiah 8:10

Those who sow in tears
    will reap with cries of joy.
Those who go forth weeping,
    carrying sacks of seed,
Will return with cries of joy,
    carrying their bundled sheaves.

Psalm 126:5–6

Restore my joy in your salvation;
    sustain in me a willing spirit.
I will teach the wicked your ways,

that sinners may return to you.

Psalm 51:14–15

This is the day the LORD has made;
  let us rejoice in it and be glad.

Psalm 118:24

His master said to him, "Well done, my good and faithful servant. Since you were faithful in small matters, I will give you great responsibilities. Come, share your master's joy."

Matthew 25:21

I have told you this so that my joy may be in you and your joy may be complete. This is my commandment: love one another as I love you.

John 15:11–12

And you became imitators of us and of the Lord, receiving the word in great affliction, with joy from the holy Spirit.

1 Thessalonians 1:6

My lips will shout for joy as I sing your praise;
  my soul, too, which you have redeemed.

Psalm 71:23

God Rejoices with Women When They . . .
Join with Other Believers ๑ฆ

"You call me 'teacher' and 'master,' and rightly so, for indeed I am. If I, therefore, the master and teacher, have washed your feet, you ought to wash one another's feet. I have given you a model to follow, so that as I have done for you, you should also do. Amen, amen, I say to you, no slave is greater than his master nor any messenger greater than the one who sent him. If you understand this, blessed are you if you do it."

John 13:13–17

God is faithful, and by him you were called to fellowship with his Son, Jesus Christ our Lord.

I urge you, brothers, in the name of our Lord Jesus Christ, that all of you agree in what you say, and that there be no divisions among you, but that you be united in the same mind and in the same purpose.

1 Corinthians 1:9–10

Whoever says he is in the light, yet hates his brother, is still in the darkness. Whoever loves his brother remains in the light, and there is nothing in him to cause a fall. Whoever hates his brother is in darkness; he walks in darkness and does not know where he is going because the darkness has blinded his eyes.

1 John 2:9–11

But God, who is rich in mercy, because of the great love he had for us, even when we were dead in our transgressions, brought us to life with Christ (by grace you have been saved), raised us up with him, and seated us with him in the heavens in Christ Jesus.

Ephesians 2:4–6

John said to him, "Teacher, we saw someone driving out demons in your name, and we tried to prevent him because he does not follow us." Jesus replied, "Do not prevent him. There is no one who performs a mighty deed in my name who can at the same time speak ill of me. For whoever is not against us is for us. Anyone who gives you a cup of water to drink because you belong to Christ, amen, I say to you, will surely not lose his reward.

"Whoever causes one of these little ones who believe [in me] to sin, it would be better for him if a great millstone were put around his neck and he were thrown into the sea."

Mark 9:38–42

But you are "a chosen race, a royal priesthood, a holy nation, a people of his own, so that you may announce the praises" of him who called you out of darkness into his wonderful light.

1 Peter 2:9

But as it is, there are many parts, yet one body. The eye cannot say to the hand, "I do not need you," nor again the head to the feet, "I do not need you." Indeed, the parts of the body that seem to be weaker are all the more necessary, and those parts of the body that we consider less honorable we surround with greater honor, and our less presentable parts are treated with greater propriety, whereas our more presentable parts do not need this. But God has so constructed the body as to give greater honor to a part that is without it, so that there may be no division in the body, but that the parts may have the same concern for one another. If [one] part suffers, all the parts suffer with it; if one part is honored, all the parts share its joy.

Now you are Christ's body, and individually parts of it.

1 Corinthians 12:20–27

If we say, "We have fellowship with him," while we continue to walk in darkness, we lie and do not act in truth. But if we walk in the light as he is in the light, then we have fellowship with one another, and the blood of his Son Jesus cleanses us from all sin.

1 John 1:6–7

God Rejoices with Women When They . . .
Seek to Understand God's Ways ❧

Forsake foolishness that you may live;
    advance in the way of understanding.
The beginning of wisdom is the fear of the LORD,
    and knowledge of the Holy One is
      understanding.

Proverbs 9:6, 10

How much better to acquire wisdom than gold!
    To acquire understanding is more desirable
      than silver.
The path of the upright avoids misfortune;
    he who pays attention to his way safeguards
      his life.

Proverbs 16:16–17

Seek the LORD while he may be found,
   call him while he is near.
For my thoughts are not your thoughts,
   nor are your ways my ways, says the LORD.
As high as the heavens are above the earth,
   so high are my ways above your ways
   and my thoughts above your thoughts.

Isaiah 55:6, 8–9

But if any of you lacks wisdom, he should ask God who gives to all generously and ungrudgingly, and he will be given it.

James 1:5

Make me understand the way of your precepts;
    I will ponder your wondrous deeds.

Give me insight to observe your teaching,
    to keep it with all my heart.

Your hands made me and fashioned me;
    give me insight to learn your commands.

Your command makes me wiser than my foes,
    for it is always with me.

Through your precepts I gain insight;
    therefore I hate all false ways.

Your word is a lamp for my feet,
    a light for my path.

I am your servant; give me discernment
    that I may know your decrees.

Psalm 119:27, 34, 73, 98, 104–105, 125

But it is a spirit in man,
    the breath of the Almighty, that
        gives him understanding.

Job 32:8

Great is our Lord, vast in power,
    with wisdom beyond measure.

Psalm 147:5

For the LORD gives wisdom,
    from his mouth come knowledge and
        understanding;
He has counsel in store for the upright,
    he is the shield of those who walk honestly.

Proverbs 2:6–7

Guide me in your truth and teach me,
    for you are God my savior.

Psalm 25:5a

I turned my thoughts toward knowledge; I sought and pursued wisdom and reason, and I recognized that wickedness is foolish and folly is madness.

Ecclesiastes 7:25

God Rejoices with Women When They . . .
Stand in Awe of the Lord ❧

If you seek her like silver,
and like hidden treasures search her out:
Then will you understand the fear of the LORD;
the knowledge of God you will find.

Proverbs 2:4–5

God takes no delight in the strength of horses,
no pleasure in the runner's stride.
Rather the LORD takes pleasure in the devout,
those who await his faithful care.

Psalm 147:10–11

The fear of the LORD is the beginning
of knowledge;
wisdom and instruction fools despise.

Proverbs 1:7

The fear of the LORD is an aid to life;
one eats and sleeps without being visited by
misfortune.

Proverbs 19:23

In the fear of the LORD is a strong defense;
even for one's children he will be a refuge.

The fear of the LORD is a fountain of life,
that a man may avoid the snares of death.

Proverbs 14:26–27

Then they who fear the LORD spoke with one
another,
and the LORD listened attentively;
And a record book was written before him
of those who fear the LORD and trust in his name.
And they shall be mine, says the LORD of hosts,
my own special possession, on the day I take
action.
And I will have compassion on them,
as a man has compassion on his son who serves
him.

Malachi 3:16–17

The last word, when all is heard: Fear God and
keep his commandments, for this is man's all;
because God will bring to judgment every work,
with all its hidden qualities, whether good or bad.

Ecclesiastes 12:13–14

Hallelujah!

Happy are those who fear the LORD,
who greatly delight in God's commands.

Psalm 112:1

By kindness and piety guilt is expiated,
  and by the fear of the LORD man avoids evil.

Proverbs 16:6

Who are those who fear the LORD?
  God shows them the way to choose.
They live well and prosper,
  and their descendants inherit the land.
The counsel of the LORD belongs to the faithful;
  the covenant instructs them.

Psalm 25:12–14

And to man he said:
  Behold, the fear of the LORD is wisdom;
  and avoiding evil is understanding.

Job 28:28

God Rejoices with Women When They . . .
Seek His Sovereignty ❧

Indeed the LORD will be there with us, majestic;
    yes, the LORD our judge, the LORD our
        lawgiver,
    the LORD our king, he it is who will save us.
Isaiah 33:22

"But," said Moses to God, "when I go to the Israelites and say to them, 'The God of your fathers has sent me to you,' if they ask me, 'What is his name?' what am I to tell them?" God replied, "I am who am." Then he added, "This is what you shall tell the Israelites: I AM sent me to you."
Exodus 3:13–14

For nothing will be impossible for God.
Luke 1:37

Great is the LORD and worthy of high praise;
    God's grandeur is beyond understanding.
One generation praises your deeds to the next
    and proclaims your mighty works.
Your reign is a reign for all ages,
    your dominion for all generations.
    The LORD is trustworthy in every word,

and faithful in every work.

Psalm 145:3–4, 13

Whom else have I in the heavens?
    None beside you delights me on earth.

Psalm 73:25

For thus says he who is high and exalted,
    living eternally, whose name is the Holy One:
On high I dwell, and in holiness,
    and with the crushed and dejected in spirit,
To revive the spirits of the dejected,
    to revive the hearts of the crushed.

Isaiah 57:15

The heavens declare the glory of God;
    the sky proclaims its builder's craft.

Psalm 19:2

I am the LORD, the God of all mankind! Is anything impossible to me?

Jeremiah 32:27

In the beginning, when God created the heavens and the earth, the earth was a formless wasteland, and darkness covered the abyss, while a mighty wind swept over the waters.

Then God said, "Let there be light," and there

was light.

Genesis 1:1–3

Am I a God near at hand only, says the LORD,
  and not a God far off?
Can a man hide in secret
  without my seeing him? says the LORD.
Do I not fill
  both heaven and earth? says the LORD.

Jeremiah 23:23–24

For from him and through him and for him are
all things. To him be glory forever. Amen.

Romans 11:36

God Rejoices with Women When They . . .
Hope for Revival ✍

Rise up in splendor! Your light has come,
   the glory of the Lord shines upon you.
See, darkness covers the earth,
   and thick clouds cover the peoples;
But upon you the LORD shines,
   and over you appears his glory.

Isaiah 60:1–2

All the ends of the earth
   will worship and turn to the LORD;
All the families of nations
   will bow low before you.
For kingship belongs to the LORD,
   the ruler over the nations.

Psalm 22:28–29

But the earth shall be filled
   with the knowledge of the LORD'S glory
   as water covers the sea.

Habakkuk 2:14

   And this gospel of the kingdom will be
preached throughout the world as a witness to all
nations, and then the end will come.

Matthew 24:14

A voice cries out:
In the desert prepare the way of the LORD!
　Make straight in the wasteland a highway
　　for our God!
Every valley shall be filled in,
　every mountain and hill shall be made low;
The rugged land shall be made a plain,
　the rough country, a broad valley.
Then the glory of the LORD shall be revealed,
　and all mankind shall see it together;
　　for the mouth of the LORD has spoken.

Isaiah 40:3–5

The LORD has bared his holy arm
　in the sight of all the nations;
All the ends of the earth will behold
　the salvation of our God.

So shall he startle many nations,
　because of him kings shall stand speechless;
For those who have not been told shall see,
　those who have not heard shall ponder it.

Isaiah 52:10, 15

　　The lost I will seek out, the strayed I will bring
back, the injured I will bind up, the sick I will heal
[but the sleek and the strong I will destroy],

shepherding them rightly.

Ezekiel 34:16

See, the LORD proclaims
  to the ends of the earth:
Say to daughter Zion,
  your savior comes!
Here is his reward with him,
  his recompense before him.
They shall be called the holy people,
  the redeemed of the LORD,
And you shall be called "Frequented,"
  a city that is not forsaken.

Isaiah 62:11–12

God Rejoices with Women When They . . .
Search for Signs of Eternity ❧

Heaven and earth will pass away, but my words will not pass away.

Matthew 24:35

Now the Spirit explicitly says that in the last times some will turn away from the faith by paying attention to deceitful spirits and demonic instructions through the hypocrisy of liars with branded consciences. They forbid marriage and require abstinence from foods that God created to be received with thanksgiving by those who believe and know the truth.

1 Timothy 4:1–3

But understand this: there will be terrifying times in the last days. People will be self-centered and lovers of money, proud, haughty, abusive, disobedient to their parents, ungrateful, irreligious, callous, implacable, slanderous, licentious, brutal, hating what is good, traitors, reckless, conceited, lovers of pleasure rather than lovers of God, as they make a pretense of religion but deny its power. Reject them.

2 Timothy 3:1–5

Would that you might meet us doing right,
that we were mindful of you in our ways!
Behold, you are angry, and we are sinful.

Isaiah 64:4

For the wages of sin is death, but the gift of God is eternal life in Christ Jesus our Lord.

Romans 6:23

Jesus said to them in reply, "See that no one deceives you. For many will come in my name, saying, 'I am the Messiah,' and they will deceive many. You will hear of wars and reports of wars; see that you are not alarmed, for these things must happen, but it will not yet be the end. Nation will rise against nation, and kingdom against kingdom; there will be famines and earthquakes from place to place. All these are the beginning of the labor pains. Then they will hand you over to persecution, and they will kill you. You will be hated by all nations because of my name. And then many will be led into sin; they will betray and hate one another. Many false prophets will arise and deceive many; and because of the increase of evildoing, the love of many will grow cold. But the one who perseveres to the end will be saved. And this gospel of the kingdom will be preached throughout the world as a witness to all nations, and then the end will come."

Matthew 24:4–14

Two men will be out in the field; one will be taken, and one will be left. Therefore, stay awake! For you do not know on which day your Lord will come. So too, you also must be prepared, for at an hour you do not expect, the Son of Man will come.

Matthew 24:40, 42, 44

"It will come to pass in the last days," God says,
> "that I will pour out a portion of my spirit upon
> all flesh.
Your sons and your daughters shall prophesy,
> your young men shall see visions,
> your old men shall dream dreams.
Indeed, upon my servants and my handmaids
> I will pour out a portion of my spirit in those
> days,
> and they shall prophesy.
And I will work wonders in the heavens above
> and signs on the earth below:
>> blood, fire, and a cloud of smoke.
The sun shall be turned to darkness,
> and the moon to blood,
>> before the coming of the great and splendid
>> day of the Lord,
and it shall be that everyone shall

be saved who calls on the name of the Lord."

Acts 2:17–21

There are both heavenly bodies and earthly bodies, but the brightness of the heavenly is one kind and that of the earthly another.

So also is the resurrection of the dead. It is sown corruptible; it is raised incorruptible. It is sown dishonorable; it is raised glorious. It is sown weak; it is raised powerful. It is sown a natural body; it is raised a spiritual body. If there is a natural body, there is also a spiritual one.

1 Corinthians 15:40, 42–44

Behold, I tell you a mystery. We shall not all fall asleep, but we will all be changed, in an instant, in the blink of an eye, at the last trumpet. For the trumpet will sound, the dead will be raised incorruptible, and we shall be changed. For that which is corruptible must clothe itself with incorruptibility, and that which is mortal must clothe itself with immortality. And when this which is corruptible clothes itself with incorruptibility and this which is mortal clothes itself with immortality, then the word that is written shall come about:

"Death is swallowed up in victory.
Where, O death, is your victory?

Where, O death, is your sting?"

The sting of death is sin, and the power of sin is the law. But thanks be to God who gives us the victory through our Lord Jesus Christ.

1 Corinthians 15:51–57

Beloved, we are God's children now; what we shall be has not yet been revealed. We do know that when it is revealed we shall be like him, for we shall see him as he is. Everyone who has this hope based on him makes himself pure, as he is pure.

1 John 3:2–3

We do not want you to be unaware, brothers, about those who have fallen asleep, so that you may not grieve like the rest, who have no hope. For if we believe that Jesus died and rose, so too will God, through Jesus, bring with him those who have fallen asleep. Indeed, we tell you this, on the word of the Lord, that we who are alive, who are left until the coming of the Lord, will surely not precede those who have fallen asleep. For the Lord himself, with a word of command, with the voice of an archangel and with the trumpet of God, will come down from heaven, and the dead in Christ will rise first. Then we who are alive, who are left, will be caught up together with them in the clouds to meet the Lord in the air. Thus we shall always be with the Lord. Therefore, console one another with these words.

1 Thessalonians 4:13–18

Dynamic Women of Faith . . .
Mary - Mother of Jesus ❧

In the sixth month, the angel Gabriel was sent from God to a town of Galilee called Nazareth, to a virgin betrothed to a man named Joseph, of the house of David, and the virgin's name was Mary. And coming to her, he said, "Hail, favored one! The Lord is with you." But she was greatly troubled at what was said and pondered what sort of greeting this might be. Then the angel said to her, "Do not be afraid, Mary, for you have found favor with God. Behold, you will conceive in your womb and bear a son, and you shall name him Jesus."

Luke 1:26–31

Standing by the cross of Jesus were his mother and his mother's sister, Mary the wife of Clopas, and Mary of Magdala. When Jesus saw his mother and the disciple there whom he loved, he said to his mother, "Woman, behold, your son." Then he said to the disciple, "Behold, your mother." And from that hour the disciple took her into his home.

John 19:25–27

And Mary said:

"My soul proclaims the greatness of the Lord;

my spirit rejoices in God my savior.
For he has looked upon his handmaid's lowliness;
    behold, from now on will all ages call me
        blessed.
The Mighty One has done great things for me,
    and holy is his name.
His mercy is from age to age
    to those who fear him.
He has shown might with his arm,
    dispersed the arrogant of mind and heart.
He has thrown down the rulers from their thrones
    but lifted up the lowly.
The hungry he has filled with good things;
    the rich he has sent away empty.

Luke 1:46–53

Dynamic Women of Faith . . .
Elizabeth - Mother of John the Baptist ❧

In the days of Herod, King of Judea, there was a priest named Zechariah of the priestly division of Abijah; his wife was from the daughters of Aaron, and her name was Elizabeth. Both were righteous in the eyes of God, observing all the commandments and ordinances of the Lord blamelessly. But they had no child, because Elizabeth was barren and both were advanced in years.

Luke 1:5–7

But the angel said to him, "Do not be afraid, Zechariah, because your prayer has been heard. Your wife Elizabeth will bear you a son, and you shall name him John."

Luke 1:13

And behold, Elizabeth, your relative, has also conceived a son in her old age, and this is the sixth month for her who was called barren; for nothing will be impossible for God.

Luke 1:36–37

And you, child, will be called prophet of the
Most High,
for you will go before the Lord to prepare
his ways,
to give his people knowledge of salvation
through the forgiveness of their sins.
Luke 1:76–77

When Elizabeth heard Mary's greeting, the
infant leaped in her womb, and Elizabeth, filled
with the holy Spirit, cried out in a loud voice and
said, "Most blessed are you among women, and
blessed is the fruit of your womb. And how does
this happen to me, that the mother of my Lord
should come to me? For at the moment the sound
of your greeting reached my ears, the infant in my
womb leaped for joy. Blessed are you who believed
that what was spoken to you by the Lord would be
fulfilled."

Luke 1:41–45

Dynamic Women of Faith . . .
Sarah - Wife of Abraham ✍

God further said to Abraham: "As for your wife Sarai, do not call her Sarai; her name shall be Sarah. I will bless her, and I will give you a son by her. Him also will I bless; he shall give rise to nations, and rulers of peoples shall issue from him."

Genesis 17:15–16

God replied: "Nevertheless, your wife Sarah is to bear you a son, and you shall call him Isaac. I will maintain my covenant with him as an everlasting pact, to be his God and the God of his descendants after him."

Genesis 17:19

The LORD took note of Sarah as he had said he would; he did for her as he had promised. Sarah became pregnant and bore Abraham a son in his old age, at the set time that God had stated. Abraham gave the name Isaac to this son of his whom Sarah bore him.

Genesis 21:1–3

But God said to Abraham: "Do not be distressed about the boy or about your slave woman. Heed the demands of Sarah, no matter what she is asking of you; for it is through Isaac that descendants shall bear your name."

Genesis 21:12

By faith he received power to generate, even though he was past the normal age—and Sarah herself was sterile—for he thought that the one who had made the promise was trustworthy.

Hebrews 11:11

Dynamic Women of Faith . . .
Hannah - Mother of Samuel ❧

In her bitterness she prayed to the LORD, weeping copiously, and she made a vow, promising: "O LORD of hosts, if you look with pity on the misery of your handmaid, if you remember me and do not forget me, if you give your handmaid a male child, I will give him to the LORD for as long as he lives; neither wine nor liquor shall he drink, and no razor shall ever touch his head."

1 Samuel 1:10–11

She conceived, and at the end of her term bore a son whom she called Samuel, since she had asked the LORD for him.

1 Samuel 1:20

"I prayed for this child, and the LORD granted my request. Now I, in turn, give him to the LORD; as long as he lives, he shall be dedicated to the LORD." She left him there.

1 Samuel 1:27–28

Dynamic Women of Faith . . .
  ## *Ruth - Great*
  ## *Grandmother of David* ✍

Boaz answered her: "I have had a complete account of what you have done for your mother-in-law after your husband's death; you have left your father and your mother and the land of your birth, and have come to a people whom you did not know previously. May the LORD reward what you have done! May you receive a full reward from the LORD, the God of Israel, under whose wings you have come for refuge." She said, "May I prove worthy of your kindness, my lord: you have comforted me, your servant, with your consoling words; would indeed that I were a servant of yours!"

Ruth 2:11–13

He said, "May the LORD bless you, my daughter! You have been even more loyal now than before in not going after the young men, whether poor or rich. So be assured, daughter, I will do for you whatever you say; all my townspeople know you for a worthy woman."

Ruth 3:10–11

Boaz took Ruth. When they came together as man and wife, the LORD enabled her to conceive and she bore a son.

Ruth 4:13

And the neighbor women gave him his name, at the news that a grandson had been born to Naomi. They called him Obed. He was the father of Jesse, the father of David.

Ruth 4:17

Dynamic Women of Faith . . .
Lydia - Seller of Purple (Merchant) ॐ

On the sabbath we went outside the city gate along the river where we thought there would be a place of prayer. We sat and spoke with the women who had gathered there. One of them, a woman named Lydia, a dealer in purple cloth, from the city of Thyatira, a worshiper of God, listened, and the Lord opened her heart to pay attention to what Paul was saying. After she and her household had been baptized, she offered us an invitation, "If you consider me a believer in the Lord, come and stay at my home," and she prevailed on us.

Acts 16:13–15

But when it was day, the magistrates sent the lictors with the order, "Release those men." When they had come out of the prison, they went to Lydia's house where they saw and encouraged the brothers, and then they left.

Acts 16:35, 40

Verses that Are Special to Me...

_____
_____
_____
_____
_____
_____
_____
_____
_____
_____
_____
_____
_____
_____
_____
_____
_____
_____
_____
_____

Verses that Are Special to Me...

Verses that Are Special to Me...

_____

_____

_____

_____

_____

_____

_____

_____

_____

_____

_____

_____

_____

_____

_____

_____

_____

_____

_____

_____

Verses that Are Special to Me...

Verses that Are Special to Me...